DR. LEE ANN B. MARINO, PHD., D.MIN., D.D.

# BETWEEN THE PORCH

*And the Altar*

## A JOURNEY THROUGH THE BOOK OF JOEL

# BETWEEN THE PORCH
## And the Altar
## A JOURNEY THROUGH THE BOOK OF JOEL

Dr. Lee Ann B. Marino, Ph.D., D.Min., D.D.

Published by:
Righteous Pen Publications
*The righteousness of God shall guide my pen*
www.righteouspenpublications.com

Book classification:
1. Books > Religion & Spirituality > Religious Studies > Old Testament Commentaries.

ISBN 10: 1-940197-42-2
ISBN 13-Digit: 978-1-940197-42-5

Printed in the United States of America.

Let the church rise from the ashes
Let the church fall to her knees
Let us be light in the darkness
Let the church rise...
Let the church rise

(Jonathan Stockstill[1])

# TABLE OF CONTENTS

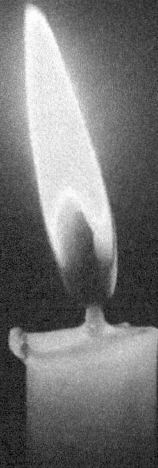

# FOREWORD

*THE* book of Joel is a Biblical text we have fragmented to bits and pieces to align its contents with modern precepts. As a result, I think it's safe to say we don't understand its short, three-chapter concepts very well. We want to give the impression that everything lost will be restored and we want to give consistent encouragement to people when they go through troublesome times. The problem with the way we approach ~ and teach ~ the book of Joel in fragments is the loss of deeper, centering perspectives we need to hear about our relationship with God and the way we are to seek His face and endure during "hard times."

Unfortunately, in a flurry of promises and messages designed to help us "feel good," we don't hear a lot about what we should do on matters of spiritual fortitude and endurance. We like the idea of moving through a stormy period and getting to the other side, with the promises of a future day and future restoration. What do we do in the meantime? What is our response when all we see around us is damage or destruction, how do we handle that? What is the proper and mature approach as believers in the Lord ~ and, more importantly, how do we hear His voice in the midst?

The book of Joel addresses these issues, and more, giving us a "how-to" guide for getting through periods of destruction and difficulty. As one of the shorter books in the bible, Joel is not a book that is hard to read, nor is it that challenging to understand. It deals with spirituality on a practical level, forcing us to look our fears in the face, see destruction for what it is, and move forward with the solid help and support of the leaders God has placed in our lives. It also gives us powerful insight into looking forward in all things, seeing God's message to us as we examine the good and bad that come along in our lives.

As people, we crave connection to others, we crave answers as to why things seem to go awry, and we crave the connections to those who have the insight to support us and answer those questions we have as we seek the Lord's insight in a deeper way. The book of Joel provides for us a layout of that connection, of the way that we can be connected to past, present and future, to our God in each and every situation, and to hearing His voice and seeing His face, no matter the time or the season in our lives.

Wherever you are in seeking God's face in your life, Joel has a message for you about that process and experience. Whatever He is saying, Joel has something to offer. Study Joel to hear that voice more closely and embrace His words to you, right now, right through to the end of the day of restoration.

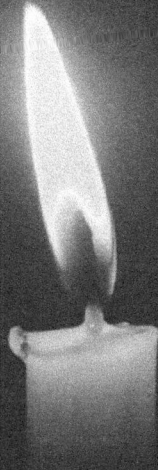

# INTRODUCTION

*About the Book of Joel*

*W*here is God when disaster strikes? What should we do when bad things happen? How do we look to the future when we can't see beyond right now? Yes, we have all heard bits and pieces of the book of Joel, especially in the context of restoration and the content of Pentecost. This little book, however, is packed with far more power than just a few assorted verses used at different times and on different occasions. It is very important for believers, for those who find themselves in-between things in their lives, establishing the needed connection to hold on through breakthroughs and see straight through to the future. For this reason, we must study Joel to understand eight key things:

- Where God is in the midst of disasters and problems.

- Identifying God's voice in the midst of disaster.

- Recognizing the role of sin in disaster experience.

- The proper approach to follow when disaster strikes, in order to hear the voice of God and discern it properly in one's life.

- Why spiritual leadership matters.

- Why spiritual leadership is important during our "in-between" times with God.

- The importance of gathering for repentance and word.

- What we should see when we look forward with prophetic understanding.

## Position in the Bible

The Book of Joel is in a group of 12 prophetic writings classified as the "Minor Prophets." Its classification as such does not mean Joel's prophecy is in any way of minor consideration or worth, but that the written volumes are far shorter than those of Isaiah, Jeremiah, and Ezekiel. The book of Joel follows the book of Hosea and precedes the book of Amos.

## Length

The Book of Joel is three chapters long. In Bibles that sometimes number the verses differently, Joel has four chapters, with the content of the book remaining the same.

## Author

The book of Joel was traditionally attributed to the Prophet Joel, whose name means "one to whom Jehovah is God" (indicating Joel was a worshiper of God). While there was some debate over whether the book contains multiple authors (such as Joel and a later scribe) in the late nineteenth and early twentieth centuries, the unity of the book's contents was established by the mid-twentieth century.

## About the author

We have little information about the life of the Prophet Joel. From what we do know, he was a prophet from Judea. He was the son of Pethuel, a man whose name means "vision of God" or "persuaded by God" in Hebrew. Even though we don't know anything about his father, his name tells us a lot about him as a person. From it, we can trust Joel was raised likely by a prophet, one who had his own spiritual experiences with God.

We don't know when he lived, but it was likely somewhere between the ninth and fifth centuries B.C. Full of contents specifically about Judah's suffering and the existing temple, many scholars place the prophet's life during the post-exilic period. Based on the reception and relevance of his prophecy in history, many believe he might have been associated with the work, rite, and ritual present in the Jerusalem temple, possibly as a priest. Others think that due to his familiarity with agricultural processes, he was more than likely connected to farming rather than the temple. We don't have evidence to support one view in favor of the other (as Joel could have written his words by both divine insight or observation), and given there are so many unknowns about him in general, we will probably never know for certain.

## Time written

We don't know exactly when the book of Joel was written. The writing doesn't mention the major world powers of the Old Testament prophetic world (Assyria, Persia, or Babylon), which makes dating difficult. Its contents also describe natural conditions that could exist at both many and any times in history. The strongest evidence does support somewhere between the ninth and fifth centuries B.C. It's also possible its contents are from an earlier point in time, it being written possibly as late as the fourth century B.C.

## Who is Joel for?

The prophecy of Joel is for all believers and offers a little bit of word for everyone: for general laity, for leaders themselves, for those who want to learn more about leadership connection, for those who want to better understand prophecy, and for anyone who is going through something serious enough to seek the face of God. Rather than lecturing on idols, Joel uses natural events to teach a spiritual message to God's people. If you desire to hear from God due to crisis, calamity, difficulty, or hard times, Joel offers a word in due season for you.

## History

The book of Joel details the disaster of a locust invasion within the nation of Israel, sometime between the ninth and fifth centuries B.C. It is hard to date because the nature of this disaster could have taken place at any point in history. It's thought to relate to any sort of disaster, including a military invasion or cataclysmic natural disaster. If it is a post-exilic book, that also relates to additional transitions among the people of Israel: the period where they did not rebuild the temple, the period of temple use, and of leadership abuses. Joel's honest examination of life in difficult times and spiritual answers to natural situations shows its flexibility and a reason why it was so well-received in its time and throughout the ages. To this very day, it is embraced by Jews, Christians of all denominations, Muslims, and among those in the Baha'i Faith.

## Context

The words of the Prophet Joel seek to give spiritual insights into why bad things happen and how to hear God's voice in difficult times. By offering perspective, insight for repentance, vision for God's Word, connection to leadership, and insight into prophetic vision, the book of Joel is passionate about its heartbeat for purpose and understanding. It conveys the power of spiritual outpouring, especially in difficult times, when believers are uncertain of the future and dealing with the trials of both natural and spiritual fire. It's deeper than it is often taught to be and provides perspective we often don't consider when we are going through difficulties.

While recognizing judgment is real, trial is real, and hardship is real, it also ultimately acknowledges that hope and restoration are also part of eternal cycles. When we experience hard times, we must remember the promises of restoration.

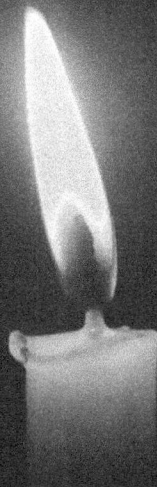

# CHAPTER 1

*Where is God? (Joel Chapter 1)*

# Key verses

- **Verses 2-4:** *Hear this, you elders; listen, all who live in the land. Has anything like this ever happened in your days or in the days of your ancestors? Tell it to your children, and let your children tell it to their children, and their children to the next generation. What the locust swarm has left the great locusts have eaten; what the young locusts have left other locusts have eaten.*

- **Verses 13-14:** *Put on sackcloth, you priests, and mourn; wail, you who minister before the altar. Come, spend the night in sackcloth, you who minister before my God; for the grain offerings and drink offerings are withheld from the house of your God. Declare a holy fast; call a sacred assembly. Summon the elders and all who live in the land to the house of the LORD your God, and cry out to the LORD.*

- **Verses 19-20:** *To You, LORD, I call, for fire has devoured the pastures in the wilderness and flames have burned up all the trees of the field. Even the wild animals pant for You; the streams of water have dried up and fire has devoured the pastures in the wilderness.*

# Words and phrases to know

- **Word of the Lord:** From two Hebrew words: *dabar* which means "speech, word, thinking, thing;"[1] and *Yehovah* which means "the existing One; the proper Name of the one true God."[2]

- **Joel:** From the Hebrew word *Yow'el* which means ": Joel = "Jehovah is God;" son of Pethuel and the 2nd of the 12 minor prophets with a book by his name; probably prophesied in the time of king Uzziah of Judah; eldest son of Samuel the prophet and father of Heman the singer; a Simeonite chief; a Reubenite; a chief of Gad; son of Izrahiah and a chief of Issachar; brother of Nathan of Zobah and one of David's mighty warriors; son of Pedaiah and a chief of the half tribe of Manasseh west of the Jordan in the time of David; a son of Nebo who returned with Ezra and had a foreign wife; a Benjamite, son of Zichri; a Levite; a Kohathite Levite in the reign of Hezekiah; a Gershonite Levite chief in the time of David; a Gershonite Levite, son of Jehiel and a descendant of Laadan; maybe same as 13."[3]

- **Pethuel**: From the Hebrew word *Pethuw'el* which means "Pethuel = "vision of God;" father of the prophet Joel."[4]

- **Generation**: From the Hebrew word *dowr* which means "period, generation, habitation, dwelling."[5]

- **Locust swarm**: From the Hebrew word *gazam* which means "locusts."[6]

- **Wake up**: From the Hebrew word *quwts* which means "to awake, wake up."[7]

- **Weep**: From the Hebrew word *bakah* which means "to weep, bewail, cry, shed tears."[8]

- **New wine**: From the Hebrew word `*aciyc* which means "sweet wine, wine, pressed out juice."[9]

- **Nation**: From the Hebrew word *gowy* which means "nation, people, usually of non-Hebrew people, of descendants of Abraham, of Israel, of swarm of locusts, other animals (fig.)."[10]

- **Mourn**: From the Hebrew word *'alah* which means "to lament, wail."[11]

- **Sackcloth**: From the Hebrew word *saq* which means "mesh, sackcloth, sack, sacking."[12]

- **Minister**: From the Hebrew word *sharath* which means, "to minister, serve, minister to."[13]

- **Harvest**: From the Hebrew word *qatsiyr* which means "harvest, harvesting; boughs, branches."[14]

- **Destroyed**: From the Hebrew word *'abad* which means "perish, vanish, go astray, be destroyed."[15]

- **Joy**: From the Hebrew word *sasown* which means "gladness, joy, exultation, rejoicing."[16]

- **Wail**: From the Hebrew word *caphad* which means "to wail, lament, mourn."[17]

- **Holy fast**: From two Hebrew words: *qadash* which means "to consecrate, sanctify, prepare, dedicate, be hallowed, be holy, be sanctified, be separate"[18] and *tsowm* which means "fast, fasting."[19]

- **Sacred assembly**: From the Hebrew word `atsarah which means "assembly, solemn assembly."[20]

- **Day of the LORD**: From two Hebrew words: *yowm* which means "day, time, year, day (as opposed to night), day (24 hour period), days, lifetime, (pl.), time, period (general), year, temporal references, today, yesterday, tomorrow"[21] and *Yehovah* which means "Jehovah = "the existing One;" the proper name of the one true God."[22]

- **Food**: From the Hebrew word *'okel* which means "food; food supply; meal, dinner."[23]

- **Seed**: From the Hebrew word *perudah* which means "seed, grain of seed."[24]

## Joel 1:1

*The Word of the LORD that came to Joel son of Pethuel.*

(Related Bible references: Jeremiah 3:15, 1 Peter 1:21)

Based on the little we know about the life of Joel, his work as a prophet probably didn't surprise anyone. He was one who knew Jehovah, Yahweh, the supreme God of heaven and earth, for himself. It is Biblical statements like this that we typically gloss over and think sound real poetic, but there is a certain level of truth within them that tell us a lot about this person. We might want to claim to be super-spiritual and deep, expounding upon visions of heaven and throne rooms, but not all prophets had the same level of deep, spiritual experience. We don't know what

Joel's spiritual experiences were like, but we can recognize his down-to-earth nature was probably different from most. The way that Joel expressed the character, nature of God, and realities that surrounded him shows a prophet in touch with the problems of this world, the truth of God in practical ways, and the very heart and face of God as God speaks to His people. Joel had a true conviction that God was always with him, speaking to others through him as a prophet. His words, and the very expressions that came forth from him echoed the heart of God in a practical way, letting the people of God know He was there for them in difficult and trying times.

This is a quality we must see in our prophets today if we desire to see prophetic ministry impact lives as it did in Biblical times. Whether prophetic messages were well-received or not, the work of the prophet was regarded with a certain level of respect and sincerity. It was understood and expected that if one claimed to hear from God, they received the proper training to discern His voice and know Him in a deeper way as the seasons of life changed and shifted, over and over again. A true prophet must know the heart of the Lord, recognizing His voice and stand back as a true worshipper of God. How one worships reveals a great deal about how much one knows about God, and the more one knows about God, the deeper their worship becomes. If one does not know God, know Him in the place of worship, then they cannot serve in the prophetic.

We don't see this today as people make a mockery of the prophetic, saying "God said this" and "God said that" when God never said any of it. Many call themselves prophets with no true understanding of the office or the work of it. Insensitive and calloused to the Spirit, they do not embrace the Spirit's leadership when it counts or hear His voice when it matters. Having a heart of worship is a requirement for a true prophet, for a person who can take us from the superficial, natural aspects of life to the deeper ones, ones that reveal what is behind matters so we can understand life better and develop a truer relationship with God.

Joel's ministry wasn't particularly dramatic. He wasn't a prophet who came before the people and called down fire and brimstone on the nation of Israel. We don't have any record of him ever working a miracle. His work moved quietly, reflecting worship. It is possible he might have worked within the temple, being familiar with the practices that went on there. He knew his work; he knew the people he was called to minister to and their hearts and issues. He shows a powerful pastoral heart, typifying the work of the pastor, as he acquainted himself with the hurt, the interests, the thoughts, and the feelings of the people who were struggling to understand what God was speaking to them and to understand why what came about in their lives came to pass.

*Then I will give you new rulers [shepherds] who will be faithful to Me [according to my heart], who will lead [shepherd] you with knowledge and understanding [insight].* (Jeremiah 3:15, EXB)

Pastors have the responsibility to care about the people they encounter, loving them through their experiences. This means they love them to a new day, a new promise, providing the hope and inspiration that reveals better things are ahead. When serious calamities and afflictions come on the people of God, it might even seem bleak from the pastoral view. This is especially true when the things that happen aren't things that believers are prepared to experience…and let's be real in saying that no matter how good someone's emergency response kit is, no matter how prepared people are with food, water, and blankets…nobody is prepared for the emotional and spiritual responses that result from disaster.

## Joel 1:2-12

**Hear this, you elders;**
 **listen, all who live in the land.**

*Has anything like this ever happened in your days*
  *or in the days of your ancestors?*
*Tell it to your children,*
  *and let your children tell it to their children,*
  *and their children to the next generation.*
*What the locust swarm has left*
  *the great locusts have eaten;*
*what the great locusts have left*
  *the young locusts have eaten;*
*what the young locusts have left*
  *other locusts have eaten.*

*Wake up, you drunkards, and weep!*
  *Wail, all you drinkers of wine;*
*wail because of the new wine,*
  *for it has been snatched from your lips.*
*A nation has invaded my land,*
  *powerful and without number;*
*it has the teeth of a lion,*
  *the fangs of a lioness.*
*It has laid waste my vines*
  *and ruined my fig trees.*
*It has stripped off their bark*
  *and thrown it away,*
  *leaving their branches white.*

*Mourn like a virgin in sackcloth*
  *grieving for the betrothed of her youth.*
*Grain offerings and drink offerings*
  *are cut off from the house of the LORD.*
*The priests are in mourning,*
  *those who minister before the LORD.*
*The fields are ruined,*

the ground is dried up,
the olive oil fails.

Despair, you farmers,
  wail, you vine growers;
grieve for the wheat and the barley,
  because the harvest of the field is destroyed.
The vine is dried up
  and the fig tree is withered;
the pomegranate, the palm and the apple tree –
  all the trees of the field – are dried up.
Surely the joy of mankind
  is withered away.

(Related Bible references: Exodus 10:14-15, Deuteronomy 6:7, Deuteronomy 28:39, Deuteronomy 29:22, 2 Chronicles 13:10, Psalm 49:1, Psalm 78:4, Isaiah 24:7, Isaiah 32:10, Jeremiah 4:28, Jeremiah 14:4, Ezekiel 7:18, Amos 3:1, Amos 4:9, Amos 6:6, Luke 21:34).

The strongest, most powerful hurricane on record is Hurricane Patricia, which hit Mexico in 2015. Before Hurricane Patricia, it was the Bhola Cyclone, which hit what is now Bangladesh in 1970. In 1975, it was Typhoon Nina, which had a death toll of over 100,000 people because it hit the Banqiao Dam. In 2002, it was Hurricane Kenna, which also hit the west coast of Mexico. In 1997, Hurricane Pauline hit Mexico, as well. Hurricane Iniki's trek through Hawaii in 1992 left that state in devastation, leaving damage of over $1.8 billion in its wake. The Galveston Hurricane of 1900 killed over six thousand people and cost over $20 million in damage, which today would be the equivalent of over $500 million. In 2008, Hurricane Ike caused $24 billion in damages to the US, with $7.3 billion in Cuba, $200 million to the Bahamas, and $500 million to the Turks and Caicos.[25] More recently, the damages of Hurricane Helene are estimated to have caused up to $47.5 billion in damages across 16 states.[26]

You might be someone who lived through one of these disasters; you might know someone who lived through them; or you might be someone who lived through a different one. Whether you lived through one or not, you likely saw the devastation of these disasters on the news, the internet, in newspapers, or some other form of media. They were so severe and so serious, they called attention to anyone who was willing to hear – anyone who was willing to listen.

Seeing these disasters is one thing; living through them is something else, entirely. When you live through a disaster, tragedy, or attack of sorts, it changes your perspective on life. It's something you need to share, something you want to tell so that all know about it, those who haven't experienced it are aware of it, and you want to make sure that others remember whatever you went through if subsequent generations come later. I say "if" they come because it often feels like there will be nothing after that moment, as if life will never, ever be the same, ever again.

The people of Joel's day went through a disaster that was the same experience for them: a locust invasion. It was so damaging, it seemed as if there was no life left anywhere. Many probably believed life would, some day in their near future, end all together. Without spiritual eyes or spiritual perspective, it looked as if there was no hope. The cataclysmic nature of the invasion was seen as a sign of impending doom, causing the people of Israel to believe the entire world had to be ending. This signified to them that there wouldn't be a trace of life left. When they looked at what used to be of their crops, their homes, their lives, and their economies, it was all unfathomable.

Does this sound at all familiar? Any time anything happens in the world, whether it be what is perceived as a natural disaster or some sort of political or social problem, the first response we see online, in newsletters, in magazines, in blogs, and in sermons and from people who have deemed themselves to be so-called "prophets" is the announcement: "Doomsday is here! The end is nigh." Every time we turn around, it's "this is the beginning of the end!" or "the end is at hand." Yet, somehow, life keeps going on, just as it did in the days of Joel.

What message should we get in such circumstances? Some things and some signs aren't anything more than cosmic experiences with sin (which we will discuss a little later). Some aren't anything more than God trying to get our attention. Some are just lousy situations that get our attention. It is easy to assume that there is more in them than we might like to admit, but even though the people in Joel's day saw what happened as a doomsday devastation, they still saw the need to relate it so future generations. Just in case the world wasn't ending, future generations need to know what happened as what was to come. Instead of assuming the world is ending all the time, we need to make sure the message we issue to the world lends us credibility and authority.

Whether the world is "ending" right now or not should be irrelevant to the way the true Christian lives their life. No matter what comes along, we should remain faithful and steadfast to the Lord, living consistently, because the Lord is with us. We should never use the Second Coming and understanding surrounding it to ignore or sidestep the notion that God is with us right now and is always with us. This means our relationship with God should not be predicated on what is to happen or what is happening, but on our understanding that God is with us; the Kingdom of God is within us; and God's presence is as real and as near as if the second coming happened this very second.

All of us, regardless of our position in church, have a place in the Body of Christ. We all need to wake up and pay attention to what is going on around us. There isn't time for being intoxicated with substances, because we need all our faculties. If we see disaster around us, that means we need to be ready to hear what God tells us next. Whether it is what to do, what not to do, or what to pay special attention to, we need to be ready, eager, and prepared to respond to what we see around us.

The locust invasion of Joel, compared to a military invasion, completely ruined the land, destroyed the vine and the crops, and caused a state of mourning. In such a state, people probably wondered what they could to do stop or fix it, as people usually do in such situations. What we learn from Joel, however, is that our responses to disasters can't be over-eager human attempts to fix things. The message, the word that the people needed to receive wasn't one of trying to scientifically dissect a situation or apply mere logic to its reception. No, this was one situation where it was time to seek the face of God – to be serious, to be open to the answers that were received, and to be ready and prepared to answer whatever comes next.

## Joel 1:13-20

*Put on sackcloth, you priests, and mourn;*
  *wail, you who minister before the altar.*
*Come, spend the night in sackcloth,*
  *you who minister before my God;*
*for the grain offerings and drink offerings*
  *are withheld from the house of your God.*
*Declare a holy fast;*
  *call a sacred assembly.*
*Summon the elders*
  *and all who live in the land*
*to the house of the LORD your God,*
  *and cry out to the LORD.*

*Alas for that day!*
  *For the day of the LORD is near;*
  *It will come like destruction from the Almighty.*

*Has not the food been cut off*

before our very eyes –
joy and gladness
    from the house of our God?
The seeds are shriveled
    beneath the clods.
The storehouses are in ruins,
    the granaries have been broken down,
    for the grain has dried up.
How the cattle moan!
    The herds mill about
because they have no pasture;
    even the flocks of sheep are suffering.


To You, O LORD, I call,
    for fire has devoured the open pastures
    and flames have burned up all the trees of the field.
Even the wild animals pant for You;
    the streams of water have dried up
    and fire has devoured the pastures in the wilderness.


(Related Bible references: Deuteronomy 4:30, 1 Samuel 3:10, 2 Chronicles 20:3, 2 Chronicles 20:13, Nehemiah 8:18, Nehemiah 9:1, Job 12:7-8, Job 26:11-14, Job 37:1-5, Psalm 8:9, Psalm 19:1-4, Psalm 50:15, Psalm 135:6, Psalm 145:15, Psalm 147:9, Isaiah 13:6, Isaiah 47:18-19, Isaiah 61:1-3, Jeremiah 4:8, Jeremiah 9:20, Jeremiah 12:4, Jeremiah 30:7, Ezekiel 7:18, Hosea 4:3, Zephaniah 1:7, Zephaniah 1:14, Matthew 5:4, Matthew 17:21, Mark 9:29 Romans 1:20, Romans 5:12-21, Romans 8:18-25, Colossians 1:16, James 4:9, Revelation 6:7)


One of the hardest things about cataclysm, calamity, and disasters is the sense of injustice we feel in response. The world no longer makes sense, and our perceptions of spiritual things are altered. Suddenly, we don't see our personal sin in the weight of its cosmic experience. Nothing justifies the devastation that surrounds us. With an improper understanding of it all, it's easy to declare God our enemy and feel as if a divine punishment is at work, one that no one deserves.

The book of Joel reflects this sense of injustice. There's no crops, no food anywhere, the storehouses are empty, and even the animals are suffering. What is there to do? How should we feel?

The first thing we see is the acceptance of such feelings. The people are called to mourn, to feel their feelings, and in accord with such, look to sin. It's this last point we will examine first.

When people start heralding the not good news (opposite of the Gospel) that natural disasters are caused by any assortment of specified sins, they do get one thing right. Disasters exist because sin exists. Before the fall of mankind, there was no such thing as a natural disaster. Adam's sin introduced sin not just on a personal level, but a cosmic one, as well. Rather than finding a harmony between humanity and the earth, the two now find themselves at odds. We struggle to tame the world as we understand it, and the world fights back. Whether under the weight of pollution, abuse, misuse, or overuse, we aren't as one with nature as environmental movements might have us believe.

In this conflict, we learn human beings aren't the only ones awaiting the final redemption found at the Second Coming. Scripture also tells us the cosmos awaits this time, too:

*I consider that our present sufferings are not worth comparing with the glory that will be revealed in us. For the creation waits in eager expectation for the children of God to be revealed. For the creation was subjected to frustration, not by its own choice, but by the will of the One Who subjected it, in hope that the creation itself will be liberated from its bondage to decay and brought into the freedom and glory of the children of God.*

*We know that the whole creation has been groaning as in the pains of childbirth right up to the present time. Not only so, but we ourselves, who have the firstfruits of the Spirit, groan inwardly as we wait eagerly for our adoption to sonship, the redemption of our bodies. For in this hope we were saved. But hope that is seen is no hope at all. Who hopes for what they already have? But if we hope for what we do not yet have, we wait for it patiently.* (Romans 8:18-25)

The struggle between cosmic and personal experiences with sin is an example of the lack of human control over the existential realities of cosmic existence. Human beings can only make so many attempts to control, change, or dominate nature (whether cosmic or human). No amount of positive thinking, encouragement, or human potential can erase sin from our lives. Therapy won't solve it. Praying it away isn't the answer. Accepting that it's there ~ and muddling through the long and hard consequences we experience through the cosmic results of sin ~ help us find God's divine presence, regardless of situation.

We don't just sin; we experience its results. We groan under its weight, much as the cosmos groans under ours. And, with no other choice, we wait patiently for the future to come.

In a spiritual sense, the cosmic realities of sin make us more aware of both personal sin and the greater realities of sin in our lives. Joel's contents reveal the realities of sin, seen by personal testimonials on a cosmic level. The devastation of the land is what sin looks like, what it does to us, and how it consumes us as human beings. Sin is bigger than all of us. We cannot overcome it by our best efforts, which we find through the Mosaic Law. No matter how good we try to be, we can't do this without God's intervention.

*Therefore, just as sin entered the world through one man, and death through sin, and in this way death came to all people, because all sinned—*

*To be sure, sin was in the world before the law was given, but sin is not charged against anyone's account where there is no law. Nevertheless, death reigned from the time of Adam to the time of Moses, even over those who did not sin by breaking a command, as did Adam, who is a pattern of the one to come.*

*But the gift is not like the trespass. For if the many died by the trespass of the one man, how much more did God's grace and the gift that came by the grace of the one man, Jesus Christ, overflow to the many! Nor can the gift of God be compared with the result of one man's sin: The judgment followed one sin and brought condemnation, but the gift followed many trespasses and brought justification. For if, by the trespass of the one man, death reigned through that one man, how much more will those who receive God's abundant provision of grace and of the gift of righteousness reign in life through the one man, Jesus Christ!*

*Consequently, just as one trespass resulted in condemnation for all people, so also one righteous act resulted in justification and life for all people. For just as through the disobedience of the one man the many were made sinners, so also through the obedience of the one man the many will be made righteous.*

*The law was brought in so that the trespass might increase. But where sin increased, grace increased all the more, so that, just as sin reigned in death, so also grace might reign through righteousness to bring eternal life through Jesus Christ our Lord.* (Romans 5:12-21)

In this passage of Scripture, we see a reality of sin we'd rather ignore: from the Garden of Eden onward, it's always been part of human lives. The Mosaic Law provided awareness for personal and corporate sin, but even before its introduction, people still died. Why? How could people die if they didn't understand sin? Because sin is bigger than any personal reference for it. We see evidence of such in the fact that calamity and disasters are all larger-than-life encounters with the cosmic experience of sin. Regardless of one's personal relationship with sin, the cosmic experience of such can still be felt.

Sin is a reality, not an illusion. We don't imagine it, and we can't wish it away. We aren't powerful enough to overcome sin alone. This also means no one sin or group of personal sins are powerful enough to cause a national calamity. Our sin might cause personal chaos (or, in the case of a ruler, corporate chaos), but such is not powerful enough to cause national or natural calamity. That position, that calamity, was done by our first parents, Adam and Eve. Today, we deal with those results, as unjust as it may seem.

Jesus' victory on the cross was both cosmic and personal in nature. Right now, we experience the personal sense of salvation, as we await the final redemption for the cosmos at the Second Coming. Despite our change in personal sin, we still live in a world that's ruled by its results. We experience and feel the results of such, reminding us of its effects in our lives. It hurts, It's hard. Our explanations don't make sense, nor do they seem to measure up in the face of disaster.

There is good news, even this side of redemption. Sin might be bigger than all of us, but so is grace. God's grace reaches us in many ways, from miracles (breaking through cosmic consequences of sin for personal impact) to the movement of divine lovingkindness through the actions of those who rise to help in situations requiring immediate assistance. Sin, disaster, and death do not have the final word. On the flipside of every calamity are those who love enough to prove that love is, ultimately, stronger than death. There is good in this world, no matter how much sin might try to destroy it. In the end, sin is temporary (no matter how long it may last), just as natural disasters are also temporary. The love of God triumphs and endures forever.

As we struggle to sometimes feel that love in cosmic conflicts, God gives us the same word He gave to the people in Joel's day: stand back, be serious, and enter into a place of repentance, fasting, and alertness to await the word and answers as to why what happened came upon them, without warning. They were to look out upon the devastation and seek a serious, sincere answer; something deeper than divine punishment (which was not the case) and something more sincere than blaming others for what they did or did not do. They were each called to examine themselves, every man and woman, and seek the Lord for what God was saying to them, about their own place in this life, what they had done wrong, and what they could do better.

We don't consider mourning to be a sacred process in today's church. If anything, we tend to dismiss mourning as a negative emotion that does not have any value and deflects from being joyful or happy in the Lord. The Bible, however, says much about mourning, and about what comes forth from the morning process.

*I have seen their ways, but I will heal them. I will guide them, and reward them with comfort. And for those who mourn, I will create reason for praise: utter prosperity to those far and near, and I will heal them, says the Lord.* (Isaiah 47:18-19, CEB)

*The Lord God's spirit is upon me, because the Lord has anointed me. He has sent me to bring good news to the poor, to bind up the brokenhearted, to proclaim release for captives, and liberation for prisoners, to proclaim the year of the Lord's favor and a day of vindication for our God, to comfort all who mourn, to provide for Zion's mourners, to give them a crown in place of ashes, oil of joy in place of mourning, a mantle of praise in place of discouragement. They will be called Oaks of Righteousness, planted by the Lord to glorify Himself.* (Isaiah 61:1-3, CEB)

*Women, hear the Lord's word. Listen closely to the word from His mouth: teach your daughters to mourn; teach each other to grieve.* (Jeremiah 9:20, CEB)

*Blessed and enviably happy [with a happiness produced by the experience of God's favor and especially conditioned by the revelation of His matchless grace] are those who mourn, for they shall be comforted! (Matthew 5:4, AMPC)*

*Cry out in sorrow, mourn, and weep! Let your laughter become mourning and your joy become sadness. (James 4:9, CEB)*

The truth about mourning is that it is often accompanied by sadness, but it also opens the door for a deeper, more profound understanding of spiritual revelation. What ultimately comes from mourning is both the comfort and blessing of the Lord, which brings the revelation of hope and healing with it. It makes us more self-aware, purposed and ready to address the issues in our lives where we are missing God. If we don't first acknowledge these areas, we cannot rightly address and change them within ourselves.

The Lord does not call us to attempt to cover up that which keeps us from Him with spiritual states and pseudo-depth that looks like something it is not, in reality, of benefit. Thus, we come to the true revelation of the assembly that Joel called Israel to undertake. The aim of every assembly, of every convocation, of every gathering of the saints should be to seek the face of God, and find Him more profoundly for ourselves.

While not every assembly is as solemn as the one held in Joel, maybe instead of trying to be cute and materialistic in our events, we should seek the face of God and pay attention to receive the answers we claim to seek. We complain and gripe about the state of Christianity today, but we still want to receive personal empowerments and self-esteem messages when such will not help us get to the place we need to be to find the freedom and understanding we say we want to have. We should call for prayer and fasting when things happen, not to try and get God to move, but to try and get each and every one of us to look at ourselves. There are just some times when worrying about how happy we are ~ or we are not ~ is simply inappropriate. To come up higher, to assess spiritual things more spiritually, is not a process that always feels like a personal pat on the back, and that means as we go through spiritual things and spiritual depths, we cannot reject the stretching, the pressing, and the growing that comes because of difficult circumstances that demand serious thought, prayer, and attention.

The Bible teaches us that God speaks to us through nature in different ways.

*But ask now the beasts, and they shall teach thee; and the fowls of the air, and they shall tell thee: Or speak to the earth, and it shall teach thee: and the fishes of the sea shall declare unto thee.* (Job 12:7-8, KJV)

*Heaven's pillars shook, terrified by His blast. By His power he stilled the Sea; split Rahab with His cleverness. Due to His wind, heaven became clear; His hand split the fleeing serpent. Look, these are only the outer fringe of His ways; we hear only a whispered word about Him. Who can understand His thunderous power?* (Job 26:11-14, CEB)

*At this my heart pounds and leaps from its place. Listen! Listen to the roar of His voice, to the rumbling that comes from His mouth. He unleashes His lightning beneath the whole heaven and sends it to the ends of the earth. After that comes the sound of His roar; He thunders with His majestic voice. When His voice resounds, He holds nothing back. God's voice thunders in marvelous ways; He does great things beyond our understanding.* (Job 37:1-5)

*Lord our Lord, Your Name is the most wonderful [how majestic is your] Name in all the earth!* (Psalm 8:9, EXB)

*The heavens declare the glory of God; the skies proclaim the work of His hands. Day after day they pour forth speech; night after night they display knowledge. They have no speech, they use no words; no sound is heard from them. Yet their voice goes out into all the earth, their words to the ends of the world. Psalm 19:1-4)*

*The Lord does what He pleases, in heaven and on earth, in the seas and the deep oceans. (Psalm 135:6, EXB)*

*For since the creation of the world God's invisible qualities – His eternal power and divine nature – have been clearly seen, being understood from what has been made, so that people are without excuse. (Romans 1:20)*

*Through His power [In Him; or By Him] all things were created [John 1:3; Heb. 1:2]—things in heaven and on earth, things seen and unseen, all powers [or heavenly authorities; thrones], authorities [dominions; kingdoms], lords [rulers], and rulers [authorities; these four may refer to angelic hierarchies, or to earthly and heavenly rulers]. All things were created through Christ and for Christ. (Colossians 1:16, EXB)*

No matter what someone might believe about global warming, modern-day prophecy, or hearing from God in this hour, all of us can agree on the fact that God speaks through nature. He created it; it remains His (regardless of what anyone might think to the contrary), here for our use and our purposes. Such demands we handle it with respect and loving care. Being good ecological stewards shows a proper respect for what He speaks and tells us through His creation. Whenever something happens, even something as cataclysmic as the incident in Joel (that caused the groaning and attention of creation on several levels), we need to call upon God and pay attention. Here is a place – not the only one, but definitely one of them – where we are called to listen intently. It is the incarnation of a period whereas we say, "Speak Lord, Your servants are listening." (1 Samuel 3:10)

Any one of us can try and give natural explanations to the things that happen, but it takes a truly dedicated group who are attuned to hear the things of God to listen through what happens and cry out to Him. If we are out of order, we need to attune ourselves to recognize that so we can resume order again, hearing from God and standing before Him in right relationship. Instead of trying to assign blame, assign explanation, or sidestep the things that go on in our world, we need to quiet ourselves down, pray, seek His face, and recognize that some things only come about through prayer and fasting (Matthew 17:21, Mark 9:29).

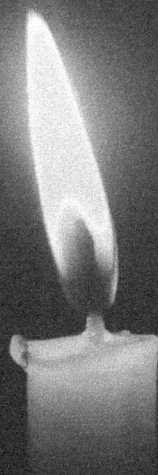

# CHAPTER 2

*Standing in the in-Between (Joel Chapter 2)*

## Key verses

- **Verses 1-2**: *Blow the trumpet in Zion; sound the alarm on My holy hill. Let all who live in the land tremble, for the day of the LORD is coming. It is close at hand – a day of darkness and gloom, a day of clouds and blackness. Like dawn spreading across the mountains a large and mighty army comes, such as never was of old nor ever will be in ages to come.*

- **Verse 11**: *The LORD thunders at the head of His army: His forces are beyond number, and mighty are those who obey His command. The day of the LORD is great; it is dreadful. Who can endure it?*

- **Verse 13**: *Rend your heart and not your garments. Return to the LORD your God, for He is gracious and compassionate, slow to anger and abounding in love, and He relents from sending calamity.*

- **Verses 15-17**: *Blow the trumpet in Zion, declare a holy fast, call a sacred assembly. Gather the people, consecrate the assembly; bring together the elders, gather the children, those nursing at the breast. Let the bridegroom leave his room and the bride her chamber. Let the priests, who minister before the LORD, weep between the temple porch and the altar. Let them say, "Spare Your people, O LORD. Do not make Your inheritance an object of scorn, a byword among the nations. Why should they say among the peoples, 'Where is their God?'"* (1984 version)

- **Verses 28-29**: *"And afterward, I will pour out My Spirit on all people. Your sons and daughters will prophesy, your old men will dream dreams, your young men will see visions. Even on my servants, both men and women, I will pour out My Spirit in those days."*

# Words and phrases to know

- **Trumpet**: From the Hebrew word *showphar* which means "horn, ram's horn."[1]

- **Zion**: From the Hebrew word *Tsiyown* which means "Zion = "parched place;" another name for Jerusalem especially in the prophetic books."[2]

- **Alarm**: From the Hebrew word *ruwa`* which means "to shout, raise a sound, cry out, give a blast; destroyed."[3]

- **Tremble**: From the Hebrew word *ragaz* which means "tremble, quake, rage, quiver, be agitated, be excited, be perturbed."[4]

- **Darkness**: From the Hebrew word *choshek* which means "darkness, obscurity."[5]

- **Gloom**: From the Hebrew word *'aphelah* which means "darkness, gloominess, calamity; wickedness."[6]

- **Clouds**: From the Hebrew word *`anan* which means "cloud, cloudy, cloud-mass."[7]

- **Dawn**: From the Hebrew word *shachar* which means "dawn."[8]

- **Flame**: From the Hebrew word *lehabah* which means "flame; tip of weapon, point, head of spear."[9]

- **Garden of Eden**: From two Hebrew words: *gan* which means "garden, enclosure"[10] and `*Eden* which means "Eden= "pleasure;" the first habitat of man after the creation; site unknown; a Gershonite Levite, son of Joah in the days of king Hezekiah of Judah"[11]

- **Desert waste**: From two Hebrew words: *shemamah* which means "devastation, waste, desolation"[12] and *midbar* which means "wilderness, pasture, uninhabited land, wilderness; mouth."[13]

- **Anguish**: From the Hebrew word *chuwl* which means "to twist, whirl, dance, writhe, fear, tremble, travail, be in anguish, be pained."[14]

- **Fasting**: From the Hebrew word *tsowm* which means "fast, fasting."[15]

- **Weeping**: From the Hebrew word *bekiy* which means "a weeping, weeping."[16]

- **Mourning**: From the Hebrew word *micepd* which means "wailing."[17]

- **Rend**: From the Hebrew word *qara`* which means "to tear, tear in pieces."[18]

- **Return**: From the Hebrew word *shuwb* which means "to return, turn back."[19]

- **Gracious**: From the Hebrew word *channuwn* which means "gracious."[20]

- **Compassionate**: From the Hebrew word *rachuwm* which means "compassionate."[21]

- **Slow to anger**: From two Hebrew words: *'arek* which means "long (pinions); patient, slow to anger"[22] and *'aph* which means "nostril, nose, face; anger."[23]

- **Abounding in love**: From two Hebrew words: *rab* which means "much, many, great; captain, chief"[24] and *checed* which means "goodness, kindness, faithfulness; a reproach, shame."[25]

- **Pity**: From the Hebrew word *nacham* which means "to be sorry, console oneself, repent, regret, comfort, be comforted."[26]

- **Blessing**: From the Hebrew word *berakah* which means "blessing; (source of) blessing; blessing, prosperity; blessing, praise of God; a gift, present; treaty of peace."[27]

- **Porch**: From the Hebrew word *'uwlam* which means "porch, in Solomon's temple."[28]

- **Altar**: From the Hebrew word *mizbeach* which means "altar."[29]

- **Jealous**: From the Hebrew word *qana'* which means "to envy, be jealous, be envious, be zealous."[30]

- **Glad**: From the Hebrew word *giyl* which means "to rejoice, exult, be glad."[31]

- **Restore**: From the Hebrew word *shalam* which means "to be in a covenant of peace, be at peace; to be complete, be sound."[32]

- **Spirit**: From the Hebrew word *ruwach* which means "wind, breath, mind, spirit."[33]

- **Prophesy**: From the Hebrew word *naba'* which means "to prophesy."[34]

- **Dream**: From the Hebrew word *chalowm* which means "dream, dream (ordinary), dream (with prophetic meaning)."[35]

- **Visions**: From the Hebrew word *chizzayown* which means "vision."[36]

- **Servants**: From the Hebrew word *`ebed* which means "slave, servant."[37]

- **Pour out**: From the Hebrew word *shaphak* which means "to pour, pour out, spill."[38]

- **Wonders**: From the Hebrew word *mowpheth* which means "wonder, sign, miracle, portent."[39]

- **Deliverance**: From the Hebrew word *peleytah* which means "escape, deliverance."[40]

- **Survivors**: From the Hebrew word *sariyd* which means "survivor, remnant, that which is left."[41]

## Joel 2:1-11

*Blow the trumpet in Zion;*
*sound the alarm on My holy hill.*

*Let all who live in the land tremble,*
*  for the day of the LORD is coming.*
*It is close at hand —*
*  a day of darkness and gloom,*
*  a day of clouds and blackness.*
*Like dawn spreading across the mountains*
*  a large and mighty army comes,*
*such as never was in ancient times*
*  nor ever will be in ages to come.*

*Before them a fire devours,*
*  behind them a flame blazes.*
*Before them the land is like the garden of Eden,*
*  behind them, a desert waste —*
*  nothing escapes them.*
*They have the appearance of horses;*
*  they gallop along like cavalry.*
*With a noise like that of chariots*
*  they leap over the mountaintops,*
*like a crackling fire consuming stubble,*
*  like a mighty army drawn up for battle.*

*At the sight of them, nations are in anguish;*
*  every face turns pale.*

*They charge like warriors;*
  *they scale walls like soldiers.*
*They all march in line,*
  *not swerving from their course.*
*They do not jostle each other;*
  *each marches straight ahead.*
*They plunge through defenses*
  *without breaking ranks.*
*They rush upon the city;*
  *they run along the wall.*
*They climb into the houses;*
  *like thieves they enter through the windows.*

*Before them the earth shakes,*
  *the sky trembles,*
*the sun and moon are darkened,*
  *and the stars no longer shine.*
*The LORD thunders*
  *at the head of His army;*
*His forces are beyond number,*
  *and mighty is the army that obeys His command.*
*The day of the LORD is great;*
  *it is dreadful.*
  *Who can endure it?*

(Related Bible references: Genesis 2:8, Exodus 26-28, 1 Kings 6:3-10, 1 Kings 7:23-26, 2 Chronicles 3:4, 2 Chronicles 9:7, Psalm 46:6, Proverbs 30:27, Jeremiah 4:5, Jeremiah 4:28, Jeremiah 13:16, Jeremiah 19:14, Jeremiah 30:7, Ezekiel 33:3, Hosea 14:1, Amos 3:6, Amos 5:18, Amos 7:4, Nahum 1:6, Zephaniah 1:14-16, Zechariah 8:3, Matthew 24:29, Luke 21:25, Acts 2:20, Revelation 9:7-9)

Joel chapter 2 opens with an echo of the intense emptiness and devastation found at the result of such a great loss to the land and to the emotions of the people. In the middle of it, however, people wanted to know where

God was as they experienced loss and suffering. This is a very typical response, especially from those who are still growing in their faith. Beyond this, even the most mature saints who have walked with the Lord for years are often left hanging, wondering "Why God, why?" in the midst of despair and tragedy, left all around them.

Most Old Testament studies focus on the Biblical tabernacle design when the Israelites were in the wilderness (Exodus 26-28). There is nothing wrong with studying such, but if we do not recognize the tabernacle was replaced and its design changed with the construction of Solomon's temple, then we often do not understand what is spoken of when the Bible speaks of the temple later in the Old Testament. The "porch," spoken of in Joel, refers to the entrance to the temple, or sanctuary (1 Kings 6:3-5, 2 Chronicles 3:4 and 9:7). Chambers were used for storage (1 Kings 6:5-10), the brazen sea basin was used for purification (1 Kings 7:23-26), courts were used for general worship (the "inner sanctuary," Jeremiah 19:14), and the Holy of Holies was the ultimate place of worship, the place where the ultimate sacrifice of sin was made.

Joel's prophecy is about what happens in the "in-between" place: between the outer place and the "ultimate inner space," the place of atoning worship and intimacy with God. This middle place, where we worship and celebrate God while seeking Him ourselves is a place where we spend a lot of our lives, where we examine ourselves and ask many of the deeper questions of life and faith in attempt to see things from a more spiritual perspective. When it comes to the world of disasters, we find ourselves squarely in this type of "in-between" place, where we are trying to seek God and figure out what exactly it is that He requires of us and where we have gone wrong in seeking Him.

There is nothing wrong with being in a place that's "between the porch and the altar." It's hard to look around life, around any state of it, and not wonder from time to time what is going on or where is God in the middle of whatever has been dealt. We downplay it today, looking for and hoping to encourage people to be in a deeper place perpetually, sitting at the feet of God and gaining insight into things that no one else can have. We criticize people who ask questions, who try to inquire as to where God is when things happen and who cry out to God in frustration or upset. We are sincerely wrong for this. If we believe that we have a relationship with God, then that is a relationship: it has ups and downs, frustrations, misunderstandings, and moments that are not clear within the parameters of our limited knowledge. God can handle our negative moments as well as our positive ones. He can handle our questions, our anger, our tears, our frustrations, and yes, even our figuring as we try to understand Him, and His ways, better.

Joel 2 offers us the next phase of discovery, as they blow the trumpet to get the attention of the people. This wasn't just a message or a period that a few needed to attend to; it was to call everyone to their attention. The call was for the solemn assembly and fast to begin, so the people could discipline themselves to seek God and find Him in their specific situation. As I stated earlier, natural calamities are not a divine punishment (although some people might feel that way when such happens). Nature and nature's movements are ways that God speaks to us and gets our attention so we can look at ourselves.

This call addressed the prophets to see the future judgment that was to come. The imagery of the locusts as an army, coming and laying total waste, pictures God as the head of that army, at the very helm of what was happening. Some might question why God would be used to picture something so vile and destructive, but those who know the Lord realize that good or bad, God is present with us. He goes before our bad situations as well as our good ones, and He is present there, leading and guiding us through the states that we encounter that are both difficult and destructive. We should never view God as far off, distant, uncaring, or uninvolved with the things that happen; instead, we should attune ourselves to hear from Him and seek His face in each and every situation such as that, right up until the final time.

In all prophecy we find three different layers of understanding. There is the immediate context, which is for the people who directly receive the message (we could explain this as the literal understanding). There is the futuristic context, which understands that prophecy also relates to what will happen in the future, sometimes in a different sense that is not literal, but can apply to what is to come later. Then there is the context that understands prophecy to apply for all time, bringing understanding to a variety of situations we may encounter and experience. These different applications of prophecy are what give us the ability to see now, later, and always through God's Word; it is what gives His Word power to us; and what gives us insight for eternity, no matter what aspect of a prophecy we are a part of; receiving it now, receiving it later, or receiving it always.

## Joel 2:12-17

*"Even now," declares the LORD,*
 *"return to Me with all your heart,*
 *with fasting and weeping and mourning."*

*Rend your heart*
 *and not your garments.*
*Return to the LORD your God,*
 *for He is gracious and compassionate,*
*slow to anger and abounding in love,*
 *and He relents from sending calamity.*
*Who knows? He may turn and have pity*
 *and leave behind a blessing –*
*grain offerings and drink offerings*
 *for the LORD your God.*

*Blow the trumpet in Zion,*

*declare a holy fast,*
  *call a sacred assembly.*
*Gather the people,*
  *consecrate the assembly;*
*bring together the elders,*
  *gather the children,*
  *those nursing at the breast.*
*Let the bridegroom leave his room*
  *and the bride her chamber.*
*Let the priests, who minister before the LORD,*
  *weep between the temple porch and the altar.*
*Let them say, "Spare Your people, O LORD.*
  *Do not make Your inheritance an object of scorn,*
  *a byword among the nations.*
*Why should they say among the peoples,*
  *'Where is their God?'"* (1984 edition)

(Related Bible references: Genesis 37:34, Genesis 43:30, Exodus 19:10, Deuteronomy 31:12, 1 Samuel 7:6, 2 Chronicles 7:9, 2 Chronicles 20:3, Nehemiah 1:4, Psalm 34:15, Psalm 34:18, Psalm 44:14, Psalm 35:13-14, Psalm 51:17, Psalm 56:8, Psalm 79:10, Psalm 86:15, Psalm 103:8, Psalm 106:45, Psalm 115:2, Ecclesiastes 3:4, Isaiah 4:5-6, Isaiah 22:12, Isaiah 53:6-12, Isaiah 57:15, Isaiah 58:3-7, Isaiah 59:11-16, Isaiah 61:2-3, Jeremiah 36:9, Hosea 12:6, Hosea 14:1, Micah 7:10, Nahum 1:3, Zephaniah 2:3, Matthew 5:4, Matthew 6:16-18, John 11:33-35, 1 Corinthians 7:5, 2 Corinthians 1:3-5, Hebrews 7:22-28, James 4:9, 1 Peter 4:8, 1 John 4:18, Revelation 21:4)

Amid despair and heartache, God calls the people to return to Him. Instead of putting on a good exterior show (that one that we are all so good at performing), God wants us to genuinely turn to Him and seek Him. Turn our heads, our hearts, our minds, and our thoughts to God, because He IS gracious, compassionate, slow to anger and abounding in love, and He relents from sending calamities our way out of vengeance or anger. In seeking God, we find the truth about Him that was there all along: the love of God, His merciful nature that is always with us, and the truth that He has never left us. If we will only stop looking so much at our situations and what is happening to us in the immediate, we discover a kind and loving Father, waiting with open arms to stand as our comforter and consoler through the disasters that we experience as a part of life.

To get to this point, we must return to Him. Oftentimes we don't turn to God or seek Him sincerely without some sort of disaster or problem in our lives. We must genuinely and honestly examine ourselves to see where we have wandered away from Him, because in some way in all of our lives, we have. We have overlooked our relationship with Him and the needed time and attention He deserves in our lives. We let other things get so important and overwhelming to us that we forget to see the inner place, the place of worship, is within us the entire time.

If we are away from God, what are our steps to return? Joel identifies three key areas that help us reconnect to God, and those areas are fasting, weeping, and mourning.

- **Fasting**: In Biblical times, fasting was always done from food, water, or both. These were not necessarily the only things people would fast from, however. It was generally understood that if someone was fasting, they were also to abstain from whatever social entertainments existed, things classified as pleasures, and sexual activity (Isaiah 58:3-7, Matthew 6:16-18, 1 Corinthians 7:5). Because social activities were more limited, there were only so many things regarded as "pleasures" to abstain from. The basic principle behind a fast was to remove distractions, to remove things from one's life that might hinder their ability to hear from God; to remove temptations, and to see more clearly from a spiritual perspective. This means that a "fast" does not necessarily have to be from food or water, but can be from anything that we know, beyond the shadow of a doubt, is clouding our spiritual vision and our good judgment, causing us to be distracted in focus. Thus, when it comes to fasting, assuming that you should fast in the traditional sense may cause you to continue to miss what God is trying to tell you. This is important because many of the fasts that we see practiced in church do not even exist in a Biblical understanding, such as the Daniel fast (Daniel did fast, but not in the way the Daniel fast is constructed) or the David fast (we have no evidence David ever did a "juice fast.") It is also relevant because fasting is often used by people as a dietary aid, in an effort to lose weight (people can avoid eating all day long and it have nothing to do with spiritual sacrifice or bringing them closer to God), when true fasting in a spiritual sense is not ever used for this purpose.

Some ideas for a good fast include:

- Media fast (no television, radio, internet, social media, or cell phones)
- Social media fast (no Facebook, Instagram, Twitter, etc.)
- Sweets fast (no refined sugar or artificial sweeteners)
- Discipline fast (discipline yourself to complete something God has instructed you to do, such as write a book, in place of spending time doing something less profitable)
- Noise fast (commit to spend so many hours in quiet or silence, rather than spending your days in so much noise)
- Varied fast (mix up what you do in a fast by combining different aspects of a fast for different periods of time)

- **Weeping**: We associate weeping with endings, sorrow, death, and ailments, because that is when someone cries to the point of weeping (John 11:33-35). Weeping is different from a temper tantrum or just being a little sad about something. Weeping is a purification process, something that we experience when we finally confront the thing that is holding us back, keeping us where we were, alienating us from God and from one another (Genesis 43:30, Psalm 34:15, Psalm 56:8, Ecclesiastes 3:4). Weeping is an emotional baptism of sorts, something that seeks the release of God as we finally release whatever it is to Him through our state of awareness and mourning (Revelation 21:4).

- **Mourning**: I spoke on mourning in chapter 1, and here I will reiterate some of what was stated there to expand upon it. We associate mourning with endings, with negativity, and with death. In a certain sense, mourning is usually an end of something, but this does not mean that mourning is negative. If weeping is the realization, the emotional baptism, then mourning becomes the healing aspect of the process, the state of realization, and the place where we unite ourselves to God to seek His face (Nehemiah 1:4, Psalm 34:18, Psalm 35:13-14). Mourning is our spiritual communion with God, because in it, we unite ourselves to Him and partake of His spiritual bread and water, so we will receive from Him what we need in our lives. The result of such is unending joy, because He has increased within us and we have decreased that much more (Isaiah 61:2-3, Matthew 5:4). In a spiritual sense, mourning means we come to the end of ourselves. We grieve for the old man and rejoice in the new man, because it is only when we die to ourselves that we can find new life in Christ (2 Corinthians 1:3-5).

From this process four major things should take place, with one major end goal to follow:

- **Awareness of sin**: Being aware of all the different ways that we are separated from God.

- **Examination of sin**: Recognizing the ways we have separated ourselves from God, being aware of such in our lives.

- **Seriousness of sin**: Often we dislike sin's consequences or that we got caught sinning, but we don't really dislike sin. Instead of trying to seek the easy way out of sin and focus on what someone else is doing that seems to be worse, we must stand accountable for the sins we ourselves have committed, and take them seriously, no matter how big or small they may be.

- **Repentance of sin**: In repenting, we turn away from the sins and the things that brought us to those sins, turning toward God and away from the flesh.

- **The end goal**: To make and bring about any needed change in one's life, no matter how important or unimportant it may feel to us.

If something is keeping us from God, then that thing has become an avenue of sin in our lives. It doesn't matter what it is. It might not even be the things that we often list as issues pertaining to sin in our lives. We might be dealing with idolatry of our families or other loved ones, or trying to compromise the integrity of ourselves to make a name for us in ministry, or perhaps chasing after money because we think if we only had more of it, we could do so much more on God's behalf. Anything can be used to separate us from God, just as doing without some of these things can help us find Him in a deeper way in our lives.

God calls His people to return to Him. While the specific details of the fast, weeping, and mourning may vary from exactly what happened in the book of Joel, God has a word for His people who have wandered far from Him, who are missing His face during their crisis. Every single one of us ~ all of us ~ can improve something in our relationship with God. None of us have arrived and we all must examine ourselves to see where we are going and where we will wind up with Him. God is always gracious and willing to forgive us when we have gone wayward, and we truly seek His face.

Thus, we learn from Joel 2 the proper format to call forth a sacred assembly:

- Call the people
- Set it apart (Consecrate the assembly to be something set apart and different, something to bring change)
- Let the leaders stand in an intercessory function for the people and their sins, and their needs before God

With all people called to repentance, we see the work of the leaders to stand for the people, advocating, encouraging, and interceding on their behalf to bring about the needed repentance and change that can come only from this relationship. Herein, we see the powerful roles that both intercession and covering play in the lives of those who are serious, sincere, and seeking God. We shall start by looking at leadership, and then intercession, to see the way that such couples to create purpose and balance in God's people.

As people, none of us can make it on our own. I meet many people who say that all they need is Jesus, but that cannot be further from the truth. We all need people in our lives, and one group of people that we need are leaders. God's establishment of leadership does not mean that one person is better than another, but that we have different gifts and abilities, and one such gift is that of leadership. While we speak a lot about motivating people or turning other people into leaders, the reality is that leadership is not about turning the work of leaders into a giant conveyer belt by which we do nothing more than produce copies of ourselves.

Leadership is, in a bigger sense, about expanding the horizons of individuals so they are better able to hear and sense God in their own lives, for themselves. This doesn't mean people should disconnect from leadership at a certain point or if a leader in question is not doing their job as a leader, but that leaders have the unique role and purpose to represent God, over and over again, to those who are assigned to their ministry work.

I think we like to sidestep this basic, foundational aspect of leadership in the hopes that if we fill leadership ideas with a bunch of jargon, the foundation of what leadership is will change. If we, as leaders, are ever pointing unto ourselves, filling those assigned to us with more of us than with God, or allowing the idolatries of life to infiltrate our ministries, then we are not doing our job of leadership. No matter what office, appointment, or purpose we are called to in the Kingdom, our basic foundational purpose does not change: To make God real to those we follow, in a way that they can reach out and experience Him for themselves in their own lives.

This happens on several different levels as a leader assumes their position of loving instruction, care, and comfort in a person's life. As a leader extends themselves to one they instruct, protecting, guiding, and nurturing them from a spiritual perspective, the principle of leading someone in church is often spoken of as "covering." There are many who take issue with the term "covering" as extended to a leader, especially due to the many complex abuses that have occurred by people who claim to be "covering" others. Referring to leadership as covering does not give a leader the right to be intrusive or to extend their leadership to personal decision-making choices, but it does relate to the way in which a leader works with and functions in that person's life.

*Then the Lord will cover [create over] Mount Zion and the people who meet there [all her assemblies] with a cloud of smoke during the day and with a bright, flaming fire at night [Ex. 13:21; 14:19–20]. There will be a covering of glory over every person [or canopy over all the glory]. This covering will protect the people [be a shelter for shade] from the heat of the sun [by day] and will provide a safe place to hide [a refuge and shelter] from the storm and rain.* (Isaiah 4:5-6, **EXB**)

*Most importantly, love each other deeply [earnestly], because love will cause people to forgive each other for many sins [covers a multitude of sins; Prov. 10:12; Luke 7:46–47].* (1 Peter 4:8, **EXB**)

*Where God's love is, there is no fear [There is no fear in love], because God's perfect love drives out fear [perfect love casts out fear]. It is punishment that makes a person fear, so love is not made perfect [complete] in the person who fears [fear of punishment, not an appropriate fear of God; compare Prov. 1:7; 2 Cor. 7:15; Phil. 2:12].* (1 John 4:18, **EXB**)

When we rightly lead people, we love them. We seek to see them transformed from the world of sin, but in a deeper way than just hoping they stop sinning. We see the power of love at work in their lives, covering their wrongdoings, covering their hurts, their wounds, loving them to God's life, loving them to their fullest potential are all a part of the covering experience, of going above and beyond the call of duty to help someone transform their life with God's principles.

The visible way covering manifests is by standing with people in that "in-between" place, between the porch and the altar. It's easy to be with someone when they have reached the place of worship and they are ready to pour all out before the Lord, receiving from Him and encouraging them to push that much higher in their faith. Leaders love to be the ones who get to stand by in the victories, watching people achieve in God. It's easy to nudge them closer to the altar, when they are on the porch and desiring more. Leaders love being able to say that they helped someone discover more of who they are in the Lord and set themselves to a point where they are going to walk on that path. The real work, however, isn't on the porch or on the altar for a leader. The hard part is to stand as a leader when they are in between the two, between the porch and the altar, trying to figure it all out. It's when the questions emerge, the directions are sought, but not easily found, and when the "Where is God?" aspects of life and ministry arise that covering is the most important and most needed.

A leader can't call themselves a covering if they are not willing to cover people during their "in-between" periods. The majority of our lives and ministries are spent in-between lows and highs, in between initial discoveries and ultimate victories, and it is in those times that we need the most guidance, support, and encouragement. God has commissioned our leaders to stand in the gap with us, love us, protect and cover us, as we move from where we are to where we are going in Christ.

Paralleling the principle of covering, we also find the principles of intercession are a heavy assignment for leaders. Intercession is one of those heavy topics that many try to teach on, but often do so incorrectly. The wave of people interested in intercession has caused a literal crash on its information, with people clamoring to find out more about it, but often doing so incorrectly.

I think it is most important to understand that anyone in church can be called to do the work of intercession, at any time. The work of an intercessor is not an office, as in the five-fold ministry (apostle, prophet, evangelist, pastor, teacher) or an appointment (bishop, elder, deacon). It is also found nowhere to be mentioned as a spiritual gift (word of wisdom, word of knowledge, faith, healing, miracles, prophecy, discernment of spirits, diverse tongues, interpretation of tongues, ministry service, teaching, exhortation, leading, giving). This means that intercession must be something else, something open to anyone in the body, and something that is neither an office, an appointment, or a spiritual gift. What intercession is classified as is a function, a body of several other things that are done in the church that help us to work together as one united front, getting done what needs doing (thus, it helps the church to function).

An intercessor is an individual who engages in the work of intercession. Intercession varies from regular prayer in that it is a work that is considered a "falling in" or a "meeting with" someone or something. Thus, we can understand it to be a meeting or falling in line with heaven for the sake of an earthly petition. An intercessor literally wrangles with heaven for earth, and for earth on behalf of heaven. In this way, intercession seeks to intervene to bring forth God's justice and release His mercy in the world (Isaiah 59:11-16). The greatest intercessor of all time is Jesus Christ (Isaiah 53:6-12, Hebrews 7:22-28), revealing the powerful role that intercessors play in salvation, maintaining connection and relationship, and in participating in the work of eternity for the Kingdom.

When it comes to leadership, intercession is more than a style of "intercessory prayer." It is not something that is exclusive for prophets. True leadership intercession petitions heaven on behalf of those we lead, praying for God to reveal Himself to them and for them to come to a greater knowledge of His will in their lives. The intercessor lays them out, bridging that place between the porch and the altar, praying that transition is purposeful, even if it doesn't come out like expected. A true leader who also intercedes will stand there with them, praying and believing, as God's revelation comes forth to that individual.

It is between the porch and the altar that we see our need to weep and mourn. We come to a revelation of who we are beyond seeing ourselves as called or purposed believers. When we are waiting on God, seeking His face in diligence, we grow. We see what we are made of and how much we are willing to see of God Himself as we go through the ins and outs of life. Whether or not we will maintain our belief comes out when it's time to stand in-between and seek His face. If we will abandon God and not receive from Him, we will make His Name of scorn, confusing others because we will not seek Him thoroughly enough to receive the inheritance He has, just for His people.

Joel 2:18-27

Then the LORD was jealous for His land
  and took pity on His people.

The LORD replied to them:

"I am sending you grain, new wine and oil,
  enough to satisfy you fully;
never again will I make you
  an object of scorn to the nations.

"I will drive the northern horde far from you,
  pushing it into a parched and barren land;
its eastern ranks will drown in the Dead Sea
  and its western ranks in the Mediterranean Sea.
And its stench will go up;
  its smell will rise.

Surely He has done great things!
  Do not be afraid, land of Judah;
  be glad and rejoice.
Surely the LORD has done great things!
  Do not be afraid, you wild animals,
  for the pastures in the wilderness are becoming green.
The trees are bearing their fruit;
  the fig tree and the vine yield their riches.
Be glad, people of Zion,
  rejoice in the LORD your God,
for He has given you
  the autumn rains
  because He is faithful.
He sends you abundant showers,

both autumn and spring rains, as before.
The threshing floors will be filled with grain;
   the vats will overflow with new wine and oil.


"I will repay you for the years the locusts have eaten –
   the great locust and the young locust,
   the other locusts and the locust swarm –
My great army that I sent among you.
You will have plenty to eat, until you are full,
   and you will praise the Name of the LORD your God,
   Who has worked wonders for you;
Never again will My people be shamed.
Then you will know that I am in Israel,
   that I am the LORD your God,
   and that there is no other;
never again will My people be shamed.


(Related Bible references: Leviticus 26:4-5, Leviticus 26:10, Deuteronomy 11:14, Deuteronomy 23:36, Psalm 13:6, Psalm 22:26, Psalm 28:7, Psalm 37:19, Psalm 65:12, Psalm 67:6, Psalm 72:18, Psalm 103:13, Psalm 126:3, Proverbs 3:10, Isaiah 12:6, Isaiah 25:1, Isaiah 30:23, Isaiah 51:3, Isaiah 60:10, Lamentations 3:22, Ezekiel 34:27-29, Ezekiel 36:15, Ezekiel 37:26, Hosea 11:8, Amos 9:13-14, Habakkuk 3:18, Zechariah 1:14, Zechariah 8:2, Zechariah 8:12, Zechariah 10:1, Romans 5:5, James 5:11)


Restoration starts with humility. Humility starts with repentance. We cannot get to the point where we see restoration without humility and repentance. If there is one message we should see in the past verses of Joel 2, we need to see this. When people are serious about seeking God, God will hear them and will extend His mercy toward them. It must be done in unity and must be done with the right heart and purpose. When we have heard what God had to say to us through our circumstance, we must then attend ourselves toward the purpose and promise of restoration.

   God promises that He will send newness of life and freshness of start in our new beginnings, during our restoration periods. The people will be satisfied, and natural invaders (such as the locusts, which started the problem in the first place) will be driven out. Even natural enemies shall stand away from the land, watching in awe of what God is doing.

None of us have arrived. No matter how many years we have been saved, no matter how many years we have attended church, no matter how many things we think we've conquered, we aren't done yet. We are still here, still battling out with ourselves and with the challenges we all have within us. Spiritual growth, moving toward a greater understanding of working our salvation with fear and trembling, growing as people, gaining new understandings of God, and growing in our spirituality are processes that we will continue to undergo as we get a better understanding of why we go through what we go through and how we got here in the first place. What we have to deal with comes around, as if in a cycle. Things we thought may no longer be an issue we discover are not as resolved as we thought, and new things come to surface to encounter the first time. Far from perfect, we experience the grace of God all over again, feel His initial mercy and love, and recognize that we can't do this without Him.

"Restoration" may be a commonly uttered word in church, but that does not mean we properly understand what it is. When something is restored, that means it is brought back again, new. Even though it might have been there before, in restoration, things are started over again, at the beginning.

We tend to get really excited about the principle of restoration because it is obvious we lack understanding about it. If we are in a restoration period, that means we are starting at the beginning all over again, purposed to rebuild and to start new. It does not represent a harvest time, but of starting again so that harvest, formerly thought to be an impossibility, can one day come again.

Restoration periods are akin to our initial salvation experience as born-again believers. When we are born again, we are literally restored, literally set up again to start over and walk the walk with God in a new and different way. Throughout our walk with Him, we experience restoration, which brings us back to this initial experience when it was first new. Restoration reminds us that salvation is a process, something that we undergo with fear and trembling as we stumble, fall, get back up again, and find the promise of God within ourselves. Just as God promises the land to be made new and the future to be bright, so too we can say that for ourselves: in restoration periods, it is proper to be glad and rejoice. As addressed earlier, it's not always appropriate for us to be excited, glad, and rejoicing, but if we are reconciled to God, and aware of that by our states of being and the things He places around us, then it is definitely something that we should be happy about. We are born again; He has given us a second chance; when we have fallen, He has restored us; and we are filled with His joy.

God is doing great things for us, whether we feel it or not, see it or not, or are in a situation where we find ourselves at the beginning, in the middle, or at the end of something. In order to be repaid for what was lost, we have to first lose something. In order to see restoration, we have to first see desolation and nothingness. Too many think it wise to preach on Joel 2:25, all the while watching and hearing congregants go crazy at the suggestion of seeing things "restored." This shows that we don't understand that this point of restoration is only reached in the midst of serious, devastating loss, in the place that forces us to look at ourselves and figure out what God is seeking to tell us. Yes, God will restore and set His people in a place of abundance, but we will only find the place of restoration if we first experience loss, then repentance, and ultimately, humility.

## Joel 2:28-32

*"And afterward,*

*I will pour out My Spirit on all people.*
*Your sons and daughters will prophesy,*
  *your old men will dream dreams,*
  *your young men will see visions.*
*Even on My servants, both men and women,*
  *I will pour out My Spirit in those days.*
*I will show wonders in the heavens*
  *and on the earth,*
  *blood and fire and billows of smoke.*
*The sun will be turned to darkness*
  *and the moon to blood*
  *before the coming of the great and dreadful day of the LORD.*
*And everyone who calls*
  *on the Name of the LORD will be saved;*
*for on Mount Zion and in Jerusalem*
  *there will be deliverance,*
  *as the LORD has said,*
*even among the survivors*
  *whom the LORD calls."*

(Related Bible references: Psalm 50:15, Isaiah 13:10, Isaiah 32:15, Isaiah 44:3, Jeremiah 31:7, Ezekiel 39:29, Obadiah 1:17, Micah 4:7, Zephaniah 1:14, Zechariah 12:10, Malachi 4:5, Matthew 24:29, Luke 21:25, John 7:39, Acts 2:17-21, Acts 3:21, Romans 10:13, Revelation 6:12)

The second chapter of Joel has taken us through some amazing places. In it, we have seen devastation, sincere repentance and humility before God, and restoration. This chapter ends with a prophecy that might seem out of place, even odd to many. In the state of restoration, God promises to pour out His Spirit on all people, bring forth prophesies, dreams, and visions from both men and women.

*'God says: In the last days I will pour out My Spirit on all kinds of people [people; humanity; flesh]. Your sons and daughters will prophesy. Your*

*young men will see visions, and your old men will dream dreams. At that time I will pour out My Spirit also on My male slaves [servants] and female slaves [servants], and they will prophesy. I will show miracles [wonders; marvels] in the sky [or heaven] above and signs [miracles] on the earth below: blood, fire, and thick [a cloud/billow of] smoke. The sun will become dark [be turned to darkness], the moon red as blood [to blood], before the overwhelming [great] and glorious day of the Lord will come. Then anyone who calls on [the Name of] the Lord will be saved [Joel 2:28–32].'* (Acts 2:17-21, EXB)

We know this to be a prophecy of Pentecost, where all people worldwide will have the opportunity to come and know the restoration and the promise of hope eternal through spiritual reception from God. Pentecost was not a one-time event; it is an experience, something real and active that ignites the Gospel to go worldwide. Pentecost is alive and well because the Spirit of Pentecost, the Holy Spirit, is alive, well, and working within believers everywhere who seek to reach out to the Father while reaching out to the world. It is mentioned in connection with the promise of restoration in Joel for no other reason than it points to a promise of restoration, all within itself. The work of the church is a restoration work; it exists to bring people back to God, to restore God's people to the fullness of who and what they are called to be, and to echo promises and purposes throughout the ages, right up until Jesus comes back. We are here to experience restoration in Jesus and support one another as we await our own restorations and the greater restoration of all things, which will come about when Jesus returns (Acts 3:21).

For us to receive this promise, a sacrifice had to be made. Jesus had to die for us to live again with Him (Zechariah 12:10). Redemption is real; restoration is real. In this promise there is prophetic realization, but also the purpose that to stand to this place as people who recognize this is possible, we too must be willing to make a sacrifice to help people realize redemption and restoration are real through Jesus Christ. We must stand in that place, believing with people through what they get through, offering true hope and help; offering the Spirit of God, poured out, prophesying, dreaming, seeing visions, seeing signs and wonders, showing forth that God is real, no matter what is going on around them.

To get there, we see again the reality that there is a coming day of the Lord which is beyond anything we can imagine. All who call upon the Name of the Lord shall be saved, just as we saw here, in the book of Joel. All who sincerely called upon God's Name, sought Him in a more profound way and were serious changed their ways and moved into a deeper place. Those who truly believed in God grew in their "in-between" place, with the help of their leaders, to become the newly restored people that God desired them to be. The land might have come forth as new, but the true newness occurred in the hearts of God's very own people.

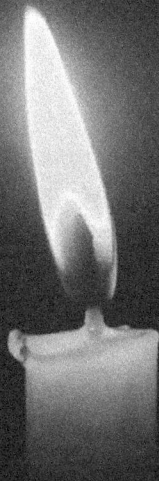

# CHAPTER 3
## Looking Forward, Seeing Now
### (Joel Chapter 3)

## Key verses

- **Verses 1-2**: *"In those days and at that time, when I restore the fortunes of Judah and Jerusalem, I will gather all nations and bring them down to the Valley of Jehoshaphat. There I will put them on trial for what they did to My inheritance, My people Israel, because they scattered My people among the nations and divided up My land.*

- **Verses 9-10**: *Proclaim this among the nations: Prepare for war! Rouse the warriors! Let all the fighting men draw near and attack. Beat your plowshares into swords and your pruning hooks into spears. Let the weakling say, "I am strong!"*

- **Verses 13-14**: *Swing the sickle, for the harvest is ripe. Come, trample the grapes, for the winepress is full and the vats overflow – so great is their wickedness! Multitudes, multitudes in the valley of decision! For the day of the LORD is near in the valley of decision.*

- **Verses 17-18**: *Then you will know that I, the LORD your God, dwell in Zion, My holy hill. Jerusalem will be holy; never again will foreigners invade her. In that day the mountains will drip new wine, and the hills will flow with milk; all the ravines of Judah will run with water. A fountain will flow out of the LORD's house and will water the valley of acacias.*

## Words and phrases to know

- **Judgment**: From the Hebrew word *shaphat* which means "to judge, govern, vindicate, punish."[1]

- **Valley of Jehoshaphat**: From two Hebrew words: `emeq which means "valley, vale, lowland, open country"[2] and *Yehowshaphat* which means "Jehoshaphat = "Jehovah has judged;" son of king Asa and himself king of Judah for 25 years; one of the best, most pious, and prosperous kings of Judah; son of Nimshi and father of king Jehu of the northern kingdom of Israel; son of Ahilud and chronicler under David and Solomon; son of Paruah and one of the 12 commissary officers under Solomon; a priest and trumpeter in the time of David; symbolical name of a valley near Jerusalem which is the place of ultimate judgment; maybe the deep ravine which separates Jerusalem from the Mount of Olives through which the Kidron flowed."[3]

- **Inheritance**: From the Hebrew word *nachalah* which means "possession, property, inheritance, heritage."[4]

- **Tyre**: From the Hebrew word *Tsor* which means "Tyre or Tyrus = "a rock;" the Phoenician city on the Mediterranean coast."[5]

- **Sidon**: From the Hebrew word *Tsiydown* which means "Sidon = "hunting;" ancient Phoenician city, on Mediterranean coast north of Tyre."[6]

- **Philistia**: From the Hebrew word *Pelesheth* which means "Philistia = "land of sojourners;" the general territory on the west coast of Canaan or the entire country of Palestine."[7]

- **Sabeans**: From the Hebrew word *Sheba'iy* which means "Sabeans = "drunkard" or "he who is coming;" the people of the nation of Sheba."[8]

- **War**: From the Hebrew word *milchamah* which means "battle, war."[9]

- **Strong**: From the Hebrew word *gibbowr* which means "strong, mighty; strong man, brave man, mighty man."[10]

- **Multitudes**: From the Hebrew word *hamown* which means "murmur, roar, crowd, abundance, tumult, sound."[11]

- **Valley of decision**: From two Hebrew words: `emeq which means "valley, vale, lowland, open country"[12] and *charuwts* which means "sharp-pointed, sharp, diligent; strict decision, decision; trench, moat, ditch; gold (poetical)."[13]

- **Refuge**: From the Hebrew word *ma`owz* which means "place or means of safety, protection, refuge, stronghold."[14]

- **Fountain**: From the Hebrew word *ma`yan* which means "spring."[15]

- **Egypt**: From the Hebrew word *Mitsrayim* which means "Egypt = "land of the Copts;" a country at the northeastern section of Africa, adjacent to Palestine, and through which the Nile flows; Egyptians = "double straits;" the inhabitants or natives of Egypt."[16]

- **Edom**: From the Hebrew word *'Edom* which means "Edom = "red;" Edom; Edomite, Idumean - descendants of Esau; land of Edom, Idumea - land south and south east of Palestine."[17]

Joel 3:1-16

"In those days and at that time,
when I restore the fortunes of Judah and Jerusalem,
I will gather all nations
   and bring them down to the Valley of Jehoshaphat,
There I will put them on trial
   for what they did to My inheritance, My people Israel,
because they scattered My people among the nations
   and divided up My land.
They cast lots for My people
   and traded boys for prostitutes;
they sold girls for wine to drink.

"Now what have you against Me, Tyre and Sidon and all you regions of
Philistia? Are you repaying Me for something I have done? If you are
paying Me back, I will swiftly and speedily return on your own heads what
you have done. For you took My silver and My gold and carried off my
finest treasures to your temples. You sold the people of Judah and Jerusalem
to the Greeks, that you might send them far from their homeland.

   "See, I am going to rouse them out of the places to which you sold
them, and I will return on your own heads what you have done. I will sell
your sons and daughters to the people of Judah, and they will sell them to
the Sabeans, a nation far away." The LORD has spoken.

Proclaim this among the nations:
   Prepare for war!
Rouse the warriors!
   Let all the fighting men draw near and attack.
Beat your plowshares into swords
   and your pruning hooks into spears.
Let the weakling say,

*"I am strong!"*
Come quickly, all you nations from every side,
and assemble there.


Bring down Your warriors, LORD!


*"Let the nations be roused;*
let them advance into the Valley of Jehoshaphat,
for there I will sit
to judge all the nations on every side.
Swing the sickle,
for the harvest is ripe.
Come, trample the grapes,
for the winepress is full
and the vats overflow –
so great is their wickedness!"*


Multitudes, multitudes
in the valley of decision!
For the day of the LORD is near
in the valley of decision.
The sun and moon will be darkened,
and the stars no longer shine.
The LORD will roar from Zion
and thunder from Jerusalem;
the earth and the sky will tremble.
But the LORD will be a refuge for His people,
a stronghold for the people of Israel.

(Related Bible references: Genesis 3:15, Exodus 14:14, Numbers 32:27, Deuteronomy 28:32, Deuteronomy 30:3, Nehemiah 4:20, Job 1:15, Job 32:8, Job 33:4, Psalm 18:2, Psalm 37:4, Psalm 62:12, Psalm 96:13, Psalm 103:20, Proverbs 18:10, Isaiah 2:4, Isaiah 8:9, Isaiah 11:12, Isaiah 13:10, Isaiah 34:1, Isaiah 43:5, Isaiah 63:3, Isaiah 66:16, Jeremiah 12:14, Jeremiah 16:15, Jeremiah 17:10, Jeremiah 23:8, Jeremiah 25:30, Jeremiah 30:3, Jeremiah 46:3, Jeremiah 47:4, Lamentations 1:15,

Ezekiel 27:13, Ezekiel 38:14, Ezekiel 39:28, Amos 1:10, Amos 9:14, Obadiah 1:20, Micah 4:3, Zephaniah 1:14, Zephaniah 3:8, Zephaniah 3:20, Zechariah 12:8, Zechariah 14:2, Romans 2:6, Romans 8:22-30, 1 Timothy 1:18-19, 1 Timothy 6:12, 2 Timothy 4:7, Ephesians 6:10-20, 2 Corinthians 4:16, Hebrews 4:12, Revelation 14:19-20, Revelation 19:14)

The book of Joel moves in three parts, divided up according to its chapters. Chapter one is about the devastation of the locust invasion and, how in the middle of that, they were set to seek God about it. Chapter two is acknowledgement that spiritual responses are often behind natural ones and if we want to find meaning in whatever is going on in our lives or what we witness happening around us, we must seek out that spiritual response. That response belongs both to the general people and the leaders alike, and the most important word in there for leaders is that they are to stand with those assigned to them in between the porch and the altar, in the places where we are figuring out our faith and handling many questions. A little of chapter two and now chapter three, we will see here, relates to looking forward: first to the restoration of the church at the end of chapter two, and now the restoration of all things in a deeper sense, here in chapter three.

The whole reason we are to stop screaming "the end is nigh!" all the time is because it truly takes away from the reality that, at one time, the current world system will come to an end and people will have to confront that very real reality. The more we make it drag on endlessly, the less seriously people will take that reality. In Joel chapter 3, the prophet takes the situation people were in at that moment and by using their experience, points ahead to the realities relating to the day of judgment and what it will all mean.

The ultimate message God desires us to hear, as His people, is that He shall restore wrongs incurred down through the ages. The fortunes of God's people shall one day be restored. Reiterating chapter two, if they are being restored, they too must have been taken away. Yet God promises that what we have lost we shall get again, and that whatever has been done to wrong the people of God shall be made right. This is an ultimate test of faith, as we cannot know for certain when it shall happen. Every time we experience restoration after desolation, it types this promise to come; it reminds us that it is real, and that we serve a God Who can take everything that is wrong and turn it around, providing those of us who follow Him with a reality that is good, perfect, and purposed in His will.

Joel reveals to us in this future unveiling that the people of God will be scattered among the nations. This is known as the "diaspora," and is the belief that the twelve tribes of Israel have wound up scattered among all the nations, distant from their origins. By this point in time, there has been so much intermarriage and cultural shifts that whoever the twelve tribes are is carefully veiled among the nations, working and living alongside the gentiles.

The thing we often miss in this is God's purpose and plan for His people, who shall be properly assembled when all things are restored. Even though the people of God are no longer assembled in one specific place, they are in all places. This is why the work of the church is so powerful and so purposed; we are everywhere. That is the point and the purpose: keeping His people in one place does not spread the message that all might know He is God and He does wonders to the nations. It's the same principle that it's great to be Christian among your church family, but it isn't a witness to anyone else. God has made sure that down through until everything is set right again, those who have been touched by God can be found everywhere. We now know these people are in His church, His body and His people, spreading and proclaiming His Kingdom, so all the world may know His Name. The people who are God's are spread out among all the nations because we are called to be a witness to Him, a witness to His glory and grace, and the freedom that He promises that only He can rightly offer.

It doesn't mean that this came easily, nor that it was a fun process. The break-up of God's people prophesied in Joel came about through the sins of the people, as they themselves divided up the land, cast lots for one another, traded young boys for prostitutes, and sold girls for wine to drink unto excess. They did things that, sitting before God, merited judgment. First, God recognized these sins of Israel, and then the sins of surrounding cities and nations, specifically Tyre, Sidon and Philistia. They were guilty of taking silver, gold, and other fine treasures, selling the people of Judah and Jerusalem to the Greeks, and what they did would, in turn, happen to them. The deplorable situations of sin showed that everyone was at fault, from Israel to their neighbors, and that all those sins would require address in their histories.

Yet, as we can see above, God even used the sins of these people and these nations to bring His message to the world. A long, hard, learned lesson, sin has consequences down through the ages that have taught us right from wrong right in our face, but has also been used to launch us into the perfect place within the plan of God.

*I will make you and the woman enemies to each other [place hostility/enmity between you and the woman]. Your descendants [seed] and her descendants [seed] will be enemies. One of her descendants [He] will crush your head, and you will bite [strike; bruise; crush] His heel [Rom. 16:20; Rev. 12:9].* (Genesis 3:15, EXB)

Way back when in the garden of Eden, God already knew His Son would be required for reparation for sin. God knew that His church would exist as the bride of Christ, and that every one of us would be here, right now, doing what we are called to do within His purpose. Where the issues of sin are thought to drive us further away from God's purpose, we can actually see that God even uses sin in order to bring about His plans. This doesn't mean that sin is acceptable or that we should seek to sin, but it does mean that nothing happens without God's foreknowledge, and that includes sin. What He knows, He plans for, and He always brings His plan forth, no matter how far away we might try to wander away.

*We know that the whole creation [of irrational creatures] has been moaning together in the pains of labor until now. And not only the creation, but we ourselves too, who have and enjoy the firstfruits of the [Holy] Spirit [a foretaste of the blissful things to come] groan inwardly as we wait for the redemption of our bodies [from sensuality and the grave, which will reveal] our adoption (our manifestation as God's sons). For in [this] hope we were saved. But hope [the object of] which is seen is not hope. For how can one hope for what he already sees? But if we hope for what is still unseen by us, we wait for it with patience and composure.*

*So too the [Holy] Spirit comes to our aid and bears us up in our weakness; for we do not know what prayer to offer nor how to offer it worthily as we ought, but the Spirit Himself goes to meet our supplication and pleads in our behalf with unspeakable yearnings and groanings too deep for utterance. And He Who searches the hearts of men knows what is in the mind of the [Holy] Spirit [what His intent is], because the Spirit intercedes and pleads [before God] in behalf of the saints according to and in harmony with God's will. We are assured and know that [God being a partner in their labor] all things work together and are [fitting into a plan] for good to and for those who love God and are called according to [His] design and purpose. For those whom He foreknew [of whom He was aware and loved beforehand], He also destined from the beginning [foreordaining them] to be molded into the image of His Son [and share inwardly His likeness], that He might become the firstborn among many brethren. And those whom He thus foreordained, He also called; and those whom He called, He also justified (acquitted, made righteous, putting them into right standing with Himself). And those whom He justified, He also glorified [raising them to a heavenly dignity and condition or state of being].* (Romans 8:22-30, AMPC)

Called to go to war, we are to attune our ears to the very battle cry that comes forth from it. Those who are weak are called to get strong, and prepare for what is coming, very quickly. The battle cry and the judgment clearly overlap, just as the battle of the locusts intercepted the people's own self-examination to avoid judgment. This can relate not just to the literal war that was spoken of in Joel 2, but spiritual battle, as well.

*The LORD will fight for you; you need only be still.* (Exodus 14:14)

*But your servants, every man who is armed for battle, will cross over to fight before the LORD, just as our lord says.* (Numbers 32:27)

*Wherever you hear the sound of the trumpet, join us there. Our God will fight for us!* (Nehemiah 4:20)

*Timothy, my son, I am giving you this command in keeping with the prophecies once made about you, so that by following them you may fight the battle well, holding on to faith and a good conscience, which some have rejected and so have suffered shipwreck with regard to their faith.* (1 Timothy 1:18-19)

*Fight the good fight of the faith. Take hold of the eternal life to which you were called when you made your good confession in the presence of many witnesses.* (1 Timothy 6:12)

*I have fought the good fight, I have finished the race, I have kept the faith.* (2 Timothy 4:7)

*Finally, be strong in the Lord and in His mighty power. Put on the full armor of God so that you can take your stand against the devil's schemes. For our struggle is not against flesh and blood, but against the rulers, against the authorities, against the powers of this dark world and against the spiritual forces of evil in the heavenly realms. Therefore put on the full armor of God, so that when the evil day comes, you may be able to stand your ground, and after you have done everything, to stand. Stand firm then, with the belt of truth buckled around your waist, with the breastplate of righteousness in place, and with your feet fitted with the readiness that comes from the Gospel of peace. In addition to all this, take up the shield of faith, with which you can extinguish all the flaming arrows of the evil one. Take the helmet of salvation and the sword of the Spirit, which is the Word of God.*

*And pray in the Spirit on all occasions with all kinds of prayers and requests. With this in mind, be alert and always keep on praying for all the saints. Pray also for me, that whenever I speak, words may be given me so that I will fearlessly make known the mystery of the Gospel, for which I am an ambassador in chains. Pray that I may declare it fearlessly, as I should.* (Ephesians 6:10-20)

We talk so much about spiritual battle, I don't think we understand the true reality that exists behind it. As Joel proves that things in the natural world often have a spiritual cause, Joel also proves that spiritual warfare is a powerful tool in our war with the enemy. As I stated in my book, *Touching The Church In Eternity: A Journey Through The Book Of Ephesians*:

*The catch with the way we are approaching spiritual warfare is that it isn't changing the everyday, ordinary encounters we have that are not spiritual in nature. People can get headaches, stub their toes, and kids fall off bikes for completely non-spiritually related reasons. The nature of the flesh means that sometimes people do things for completely personal reasons that have nothing to do with either the enemy or God, and we must take all this into consideration when considering the realm of spiritual warfare. The fact that these methods are so ineffective turns people indifferent to the true spiritual* enemies and realities that we must face, and the true reasons for spiritual warfare. Even though the modern-day church has made spiritual warfare a fanciful, almost laughable demon-chasing activity, Christians do have a real enemy, we have people in this lifetime who reflect this enemy, thus manifesting in the natural as our enemies, and we are confronted, every day, with these different realities. This means we, as Christians, need to know how best to handle it.

The first piece of advice is to remain strong in the Lord, and His power. We most effectively do this by remaining connected to Him, and living and loving as He commands us to do. There is something to be said for remaining peaceful in adversity, and remaining stable in difficult situations. While the world gets upset, remaining peaceful and balanced is always a line of defense. Being strong doesn't mean being aggressive; it means being able to bear and withstand whatever comes along, without being easily burdened or flinched.

It's been said that the best defense is also the best offense. This can be applied to the principle of spiritual armor, which we are commanded to put on as believers. Nothing mentioned in this passage encourages believers to be hostile or aggressive, but to use that which is available to them spiritually. The reason we are encouraged to do this is for one reason, and one reason only: the devil is a schemer, and the different powers, principalities, authorities, and spiritual forces have a way of working for him, tipping the scales in his favor. The enemy will use whoever he desires, whenever it is convenient, even those we might not expect or consider, in order to keep us easily distracted. If we recognize that some of the things that happen to us (especially when dealing with the world and the powers of this world) because the enemy is trying to get at us by using other people and spiritual forces, then we can step up and defend ourselves, spiritually prepared and ready to stand when issues come up. We are called to do everything that we can do, and when we have done that, still stand. When we've done what makes sense, what doesn't make sense, what seems the most spiritual, what seems the most rational, and nothing has worked, we can still stand, because we are ready and prepared for whatever might come against us. We are to stand firm with:

- **Belt of truth buckled around the waist:** It shouldn't come as much of a surprise that the spiritual armor mentioned here is parallel in appearance to the natural armor worn by military personnel in the first century. Armor was a protective point, and the spiritual armor serves that same point. The belt of truth buckled around the waist holds us up, as truth does in our lives. If we are buckled with truth, which keeps our pants or skirt up, our shirt tucked in, and our appearance together, then we can stand firm and upright, without shame or embarrassment.

- **Breastplate of righteousness in place:** The breastplate protects the chest area, particularly the innards of the heart, lungs, and other essential internal organs. If we allow righteousness to guard our heart, we will follow the ways of the Lord and He will give us the desires of our heart (Psalm 37:4). If we allow righteousness to protect our lungs, we will breathe in the breath of the Spirit with every breath (Job 32:8, Job 33:4). If we allow righteousness to protect our most delicate inwardness, then we will be guided and directed by God, even in our most intimate thoughts, moments, and issues (2 Corinthians 4:16).

- **Feet fitted with the readiness that comes from the Gospel of peace:** We should be the first to move with the Spirit as He guides us, moving in peace rather than hostility or anger, and good judgment rather than impulsivity. God has given us the right preparation, and as we exercise our preparation, we are ready for our walk with God, our calling, and to answer our greater life purpose. Movement in peace is a lifestyle that we are properly fitted for, something that fits us right and has us ready for each and every moment that we will encounter in this life.

- *Shield of faith, which extinguishes flaming arrows:* The enemy doesn't play fair; that's why he is the enemy, and why he has his victories. He has a way of hitting us where it hurts most, alluring us with what we want the most to get us away from where we need to be, and attacking us right at the time we need it least. Given this, the shield of faith, which is held slightly out in front of the body, is there to extinguish these flaming arrows. Flaming arrows, or arrows lit on fire and then shot at an opposing force, were a primary weapon of defense (not to mention a rather effective one) that required the opposing force to somehow extinguish them and prevent them from entering the body. A shield was effective for this, as is the shield of faith. If our faith is our first defense, it means that our trust and confidence in God is the first thing we should have around us, keeping things from invading in. When the enemy comes at us with his best shot, our continued faith and perseverance to God's plan for us is the best defense to put down anything Satan wants to send our way to take us out.

- *Helmet of salvation:* Helmets protect heads from injuries. This is important, as our head contains our brain, which controls the functions of our entire body. The helmet of salvation reminds us that it is important to protect what goes into our head – our thoughts, processes, images, ideas, concepts, and other similar things – which might easily cause us to derail off course.

- *Sword of the Spirit, which is the Word of God:* We learn in Hebrews 4:12 that:

  God's Word is living and active. It is sharper than any two-edged sword and cuts as deep as the place where soul and spirit meet, the place where joints and marrow meet. God's Word judges a person's thoughts and intentions. *(GW)*

The word, "word" is the Greek word, rhema, which refers to any spoken word that comes (in this instance) from God. The sword of the Spirit as the word of God is the proper use of Scripture and relaying God's words to us in our lives, recognizing the benefit of both as a powerful weapon against the work of the enemy. If we are understanding of Scripture in our lives and of forma of spoken revelation (word of knowledge, word of wisdom, and prophecy), we will know what God is doing in season and out of season.

- **Pray in the Spirit on all occasions, with many kinds of prayers:** Praying in the Spirit is more than just speaking in tongues, although that is definitely a part of it. To pray in the Spirit means to be in touch with the intercession of the Spirit (Romans 8:26-27), knowing what to pray for and when. There are many ways we can pray, and we are encouraged to familiarize ourselves with many kinds of prayers, so we are ready to pray in all situations and communicate exactly what we desire to communicate to God, no matter what the situation may be.

- **Be alert and keep praying for the saints:** Being alert means being watchful and prepared. In a state of alertness, we aren't falling asleep on the job, ignoring the things that are going on around us, nor the things that are going on in the spiritual realm. It doesn't mean becoming a miracle chaser, nor a demon chaser, but finding the middle ground between awareness and obsession with things that lead us away from where we should be. Not only should we be aware, but we should be thinking of others in the body, praying for the saints: for those we know and those we don't know, our leaders and our friends, our brothers and sisters in Christ, our missionaries and all who are a part of this family of faith, the church, that is walking with God in our day and age.

None of these things listed as a part of spiritual warfare involve fancy exorcisms, spitting, screaming, throwing water or oil at people, running around in circles, begging other people to help us, running to our neighbors for protection, or vanishing to hide. The armor of the Lord says nothing about covering our backsides, which means that they shouldn't be left to be vulnerable and exposed. No, we are given the ability to stand; to be spiritually aware; and to be prepared in each and every situation. God does not tell us to avoid the battle, but to be ready for it, and to expect that it will come at different times of our lives.

The Apostle Paul closes this section by asking for prayer for himself: that he might fearlessly proclaim the Gospel, and move in faith, as he should. This reminds us of how important prayer is for our leaders, those who have personally deposited into our lives, and those who benefit from that deposit, indirectly. The Apostle Paul is not the personal apostle of any living person today, because he lived so long ago. We are still reading his words, however, and gaining a greater insight into what God asks of us today because of the impact he had on the churches of the first century. Even though you may not directly know an apostle, you know someone whose life is being transformed or changed by one. Remember leaders in prayer, even those you do not personally know. It is a difficult task to be in leadership, and to constantly come up against the world. The hostilities and warfare that leaders face is intense, and it is through prayer and encouragement that leaders (especially apostles) are able to endure and overcome.

Spiritual warfare isn't about being cute or about casting out a demon around every corner. It is about developing oneself and one's spiritual realities so we are rightly prepared for anything, and any enemy that may arise. As we await the restoration of all things, we see God present in each and every victory that will find us as we continue to wait for His Word and find Him deeper in every situation.

Every day of our lives as believers, we rejoice in the truth that we have found in the decision that we've made. Joel reminds us that there are multitudes still who have not made this decision, who are undecided on their choices. This tells us that most people have an important, eternal decision to make ~ and I am sure, many other smaller decisions to be made, as well. Good, bad, or indifferent, this is where most people will find themselves, and because judgment comes near to all of us at some point in time, we need to be people who help others with their decisions. These decisions ~ and ultimately, the big decision ~ come about as we stand between the porch and the altar with others, helping them through their desires and their thoughts, and to sort out the essential spiritual matters that relate to such. While we argue and debate over whether or not salvation is eternal or can be lost, we can clearly see in the Bible that the understandings we try to attach to matters of salvation were simply not things that were presented in the text, nor are they the essence of what God wants to convey to any of us about the salvation process. The bottom line of salvation is that it is something God has done for us and it is something that we get to choose for ourselves if we want, but it is not the end of our decisions that pertain to spiritual things. The Lord never forces Himself upon us, but wants us to know that He is here for us, waiting and ready to receive us whenever the decisions are ready to be made.

When the signs continue to advance, there won't be a place to go, save to the Lord, because He is a refuge, and the ultimate place of safety. Every one of us has been in this position, and therefore, we are the perfect people to pray, to intercede, and to model the fine example set for us by solid leaders as we help others find the truth they need so they can make their right decision and change someone else's life. May we be there to stand in the gap; to decide what is ultimately right for us and what is right in the pictures of eternity; to encourage and edify, and to reveal the heart of God, at each and every decision-making pass.

Joel 3:17-21

"Then you will know that I, the LORD your God,
    dwell in Zion, My holy hill.
Jerusalem will be holy;
    never again will foreigners invade her.

"In that day the mountains will drip new wine,
    and the hills will flow with milk;
    all the ravines of Judah will run with water.
A fountain will flow out of the LORD's house
    and will water the valley of acacias.
But Egypt will be desolate,
    Edom a desert waste,
because of violence done to the people of Judah,
    in whose land they shed innocent blood.
Judah will be inhabited forever
    and Jerusalem through all generations.
Shall I leave their innocent blood unavenged?
    No, I will not."

## The LORD dwells in Zion!

(Related Bible references: Psalm 48:8, Isaiah 4:3, Isaiah 19:1, Isaiah 33:20, Isaiah 35:8, Isaiah 41:19, Isaiah 60:8, Isaiah 60:15, Jeremiah 49:17, Ezekiel 25:15, Ezekiel 36:25, Amos 9:5, Amos 9:13, Obadiah 1:16, Micah 4:7, Micah 7:19, Nahum 1:15, Zechariah 8:13, 1 Corinthians 6:2, 2 Timothy 2:11-13, Revelation 22:1)

The final words of Joel end on a note that are overwhelmingly positive. The ultimate promise of restoration is that we will know God, and we will be one with Him. We will not have the confines of sin or the problems of this world, and all things shall be restituted, because we serve a God Who is that great, that big, that relevant, and that just. We shall find the peace we crave, the forgiveness we seek, the peace that we can touch now; not fully, but in part, when we live in homes of peace, churches of peace, and as people of peace. God's people shall be clearly blessed, with clear distinction made between God's people and those who have set themselves against Him and His people, right up until the end. God's people will be clearly blessed, clearly identified, and clearly set apart, to rule with Him in His restored time.

*Surely [Don't...?] you know that God's people [the saints] will judge the world. So if you are to judge the world, are you not able to judge small [trivial; the smallest of] cases as well?* (1 Corinthians 6:2, EXB)

*This teaching is true [saying/word is trustworthy; 1 Tim. 1:15; 3:1; 4:9; Titus 3:8; what follows may be an early Christian hymn]: If we died with Him, we will also live with Him. If we accept suffering [endure; persevere], we will also rule [reign] with Him. If we say we don't know [deny; disown; renounce] Him, He will say He doesn't know [deny; disown; renounce] us. If we are not faithful, He will still be faithful, because He must be true to Who He is [cannot deny/disown Himself].* (2 Timothy 2:11-13, EXB)

Every day of our lives, we are confronted with the realities of this world: disasters, questions about where God is and whether He cares about His creation, and how He handles matters that pertain to sin and alienation from Him. We are reminded that we, and others alike, fail Him more than we would like to admit, and find ourselves in a place where we need to seek Him, once again, for restoration.

In restoration, we find forgiveness. We find the hope, the strength, the purpose to walk forward, out of something, away from a reality that might have found us, but that we don't have to find ourselves stuck in. It is only God that offers us that hope, that light, that expectancy to point toward the ultimate restoration that is coming and the ultimate life that is found only in Him, right now, real as we can reach out and touch, for us today, in this day in which we live.

We can make it from the porch to the altar, even when we get hung up by problems and circumstances in the middle, as we make different choices, both in the spiritual and the natural. As we make our decisions and claim our promises, it is God Who offers us the hope to pick ourselves up, dust ourselves off, and walk into a better destiny, one that is truly eternal, and find in Him the truth of that better day.

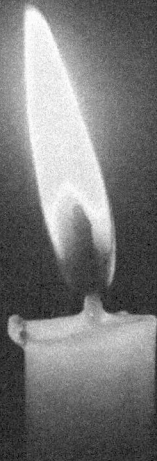

# REFERENCES

# EPIGRAPH

[1] *Stockstill, Jonathan. "Let The Church Rise."*
http://www.lyricsmode.com/lyrics/j/jonathan_stockstill/let_the_church_rise.html. Accessed July 6, 2016.

# INTRODUCTION

- "Book Of Joel." https://en.wikipedia.org/wiki/Book_of_Joel. Accessed May 23, 2016.
- "Joel (Prophet)." https://en.wikipedia.org/wiki/Joel_%28prophet%29. Accessed May 23, 2016.

# CHAPTER 1

[1] *Strong's Exhaustive Concordance of the Bible*, #1697
[2] Ibid., #3068
[3] Ibid., #3100
[4] Ibid., #6602
[5] Ibid, #1755
[6] Ibid., #1501
[7] Ibid., #6974
[8] Ibid., #1058
[9] Ibid., #6071
[10] Ibid., #1471
[11] Ibid., #0421
[12] Ibid., #8242
[13] Ibid., #8334
[14] Ibid., #7105
[15] Ibid., #0006
[16] Ibid., #8342
[17] Ibid., #5594
[18] Ibid., #6942
[19] Ibid., #6685
[20] Ibid., #6116
[21] Ibid., #3117
[22] Ibid., #3068
[23] Ibid., #0400
[24] Ibid., #6507
[25] "10 Biggest, Deadliest, Most destructive Hurricanes Ever." http://www.ranker.com/list/10-biggest-deadliest-most-destructive-hurricane_s-ever-/jeff419. Accessed June 27, 2016.
[26] Egan, Matt. "As Hurricane Milton Threatens US, Helene Could Cost Property Owners More than $47 Billion." *CNN Business*. Accessed October 15, 2024.

# CHAPTER 2

[1] Strong's Exhaustive Concordance of the Bible, #7782

[2] Ibid., #6726

[3] Ibid., #7321

[4] Ibid., #7264

[5] Ibid., #2822

[6] Ibid., #0653

[7] Ibid., #6051

[8] Ibid., #7837

[9] Ibid., #3852

[10] Ibid., #1588

[11] Ibid., #5731

[12] Ibid., #8077

[13] Ibid., #4057

[14] Ibid., #2342

[15] Ibid., #6685

[16] Ibid., #1065

[17] Ibid., #4553

[18] Ibid., #7167

[19] Ibid., #7725

[20] Ibid., #2587

[21] Ibid., #7349

[22] Ibid., #0750

[23] Ibid., #0639

[24] Ibid., #7227

[25] Ibid., #2617

[26] Ibid., #5162

[27] Ibid., #1293

[28] Ibid., #0197

[29] Ibid., #4196

[30] Ibid., #7065

[31] Ibid., #1523

[32] Ibid., #7999

[33] Ibid., #7307

[34] Ibid., #5012

[35] Ibid., #2472

[36] Ibid., #2384

[37] Ibid., #5650

[38] Ibid., #8210

[39] Ibid., #4159

[40] Ibid., #6413

[41] Ibid., #8300

# CHAPTER 3

[1] Strong's Exhaustive Concordance of the Bible, #8199

[2] Ibid., #6010

[3] Ibid., #3092

[4] Ibid., #5159

[5] Ibid., #6865

[6] Ibid., #6721

[7] Ibid., #6429

[8] Ibid., #7615

[9] Ibid., #4421

[10] Ibid., #1368

[11] Ibid., #1995

[12] Ibid., #6010

[13] Ibid., #2742

[14] Ibid., #4851

[15] Ibid., #4599

[16] Ibid., #4714

[17] Ibid., #0123

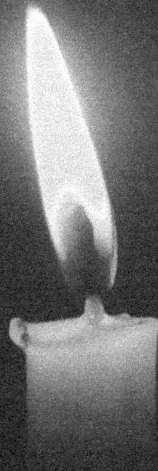

# ABOUT THE AUTHOR

Dr, Lee Ann B. Marino,
Ph.D., D.Min., D.D.

**Dr. Lee Ann B. Marino, Ph.D., D.Min., D.D.** (she/her) is "everyone's favorite theologian" leading Gen X, Millennials, and Gen Z with expertise in leadership training, queer and feminist theology, general religion, and apostolic theology. She has served in ministry since 1998 and was ordained as a pastor in 2002 and an apostle in 2010. She founded what is now Sanctuary Apostolic Fellowship Empowerment (SAFE) Ministries in 2004. Under her ministry heading Dr. Marino is founder and Overseer of Sanctuary International Fellowship Tabernacle (SIFT) (the original home of National Coming Out Sunday) and The Sanctuary Network, and Chancellor of Apostolic Covenant Theological Seminary (ACTS).

Affectionately nicknamed "the Spitfire," Dr. Marino has spent over two decades as an "apostle, preacher, and teacher" (2 Timothy 1:11), exercising her personal mandate to become "all things to all people" (1 Corinthians 9:22). Her embrace of spiritual issues (both technical and intimate) has found its home among both seekers and believers, those who desire spiritual answers to today's issues.

Dr. Marino has preached throughout the United States, Puerto Rico, and Europe in hundreds of religious services and experiences throughout the years. A history maker in her own right, she has spent over two decades in advocacy, education, and work for and within minority spiritual communities (including African American, Hispanic, and LGBTQ+). She has also served as the first woman on all-male synods, councils, and panels, as well as the first preacher or speaker welcomed of a different race, sexual orientation, or identity among diverse communities. Today, Dr. Marino's work extends to over 150 countries as she hosts the popular *Kingdom Now* podcast, which is in the top 20 percentile of all podcasts worldwide. She is also the author of over 35 books and the popular Patheos column, *Leadership on Fire*. To date, she has had five bestselling titles within their subject matter: *Understanding Demonology, Spiritual Warfare, Healing, and Deliverance: A Manual for the Christian Minister*; *Ministry School Boot Camp: Training for Helps Ministries, Appointments, and Beyond*; *Discovering Intimacy: A Journey Through the Song of Solomon*; *Fruit of the Vine: Study and Commentary on the Fruit of the Spirit*; and *Ministering to LGBTQ+ (and Those Who Love Them): A Primer for Queer Theology* (and its accompanying workbook).

As a public icon and social media influencer, Dr. Marino advocates healthy body image (curvy/full-figured), representation as a demisexual/aromantic, and albinism awareness as a model. Known to those she works with, she is a spiritual mom, teacher, leader, professor, confidant, and friend. She continues to transform, receiving new teaching, revelation, and insight in this thing we call "ministry." Through years of spiritual growth and maturity, Dr. Marino stands as herself, here to present what God has given to her for any who have an ear to hear.

For more information, visit her website at kingdompowernow.org.

www.ingramcontent.com/pod-product-compliance
Lightning Source LLC
Chambersburg PA
CBHW031603040426

42452CB00006B/397